D1034556

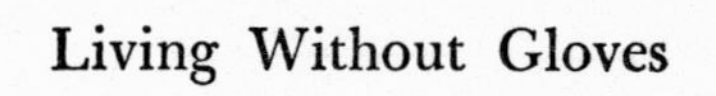
Living Without Gloves

Halford E. Luccock

Living Without Gloves

MORE LETTERS OF SIMEON STYLITES

New York

OXFORD UNIVERSITY PRESS

1957

Library of Congress Catalogue Card Number: 57-10385

Printed in the United States of America

Foreword

Robert Louis Stevenson once said that a few letters, full of gossip, would cure his cough. When he was an exile in San Francisco, dead broke and just one jump ahead of the undertaker, he made a complaint about his letters from home. He wrote:

"I'm vexed about my letters. Nobody ever tells me any news about people. Everybody writes me sermons. It's good for me, but hardly the food necessary for a man who lives on 45 cents a day. If you'd only write me a letter with some *gossip* in it . . . it would cure my cough."

These letters from Simeon Stylites, selected from those which have been published in *The Christian Century,* are not guaranteed to cure anyone's cough. But they do have gossip of sorts. They do not illuminate fixed fate, or justify the ways of God to man, or wax mighty in war on other Miltonic themes. Such things are too high for them. They cannot attain to them.

But they do have some gossip, non-malignant variety, about some minor entanglements of life. They cannot cure a cough. But if, for a moment, they may cure or alleviate any downheartedness for anyone, that will be more than I had hoped.

HALFORD E. LUCCOCK

Acknowledgements: The author is grateful to Langston Hughes, The Cresset Press, London, *The New Yorker,* and the *Harvard Alumni Bulletin* for their kind permission to reprint copyrighted material.

Contents

Living Without Gloves, 3
Hard and Soft Saints, 5
Don't Cut Off the Buttons, 7
Mechanical Half-Hour, 10
"You Wouldn't Have Won If . . . " 12
Letter to Madison Avenue, 14
How To Handle Your Correspondence, 16
"She'll Be Comin' Round the Mountain," 18
Performing Lion, 21
"I Remember, I Remember," 23
"London Grace," 25
No Time for Barak, 28
TV and the Canadian Rockies, 30
"We'll Be So Respectable—", 32
Render Unto Caesar, 34
He Ate with the Crew, 37
Jumping Out of Your Skin, 39

Books for Tired Eyes, 41
Whooping Crane, 44
In Defense of Gossip, 46
New Look in Preachers' Wives, 48
Will You Marry Me? 51
Two Can Keep from Growing Old, 53
Trivial, 55
The Constant Thermometer, 57
William Shakespeare's Ghost, 60
Drunk and Disorderly, 62
Viva la Negative! 63
Riffraff, 65
What Happened to the Kitchen? 67
An Orchid for the Weather Man, 70
Travel by the Train, 72
Pigheaded, 74
Effective Speaking for Wives, 77
A Plea for Disorderly Conduct, 79
A Growl from the Pew, 82
The Cult of the Hairy Ape, 84
Tiddlywinks, 86
"I've Got a Little List," 89
King of Indoor Sports, 91
Coldness of Mind, 94
Pilate's Washbowl, 96
The Pastor in Greek Mythology, 98
"A Screech of Some Kind," 101
The Hour-a-Day Work Week, 103
"Know-How," 105
The Big Bores, 108

Assets of Doubtful Value, 111
Consider the Corncrake, 114
The Human Face Divine, 116
She Sits in the Seventh Row, 119
Take A Shopping Trip, 121
John Wesley—Revised, 123
On the Surface, 126
"I Wanted To Go Home," 129
Salute to Librarians, 132
Consider the Duck, 134
Red Ink, 136
I Am Elected Secretary, 138
The Church of St. Demas, 141
"Old Fuss and Feathers," 143
"At Home in Any Cemetery," 145
"Stout Cortez," 148
"Fourscore and Seven Years Ago," 151
The Power of Negative Thinking, 153
Cucumber Sandwich, 155
What Is Your Fog Index? 158
The Grace of Receiving, 160
The Inside Story, 163
The Devils Were White, 165
Broadcasting A Quaker Meeting, 167
"Take Me Out to the Ball Game," 170
The Wail of a Duffer, 172
New Christian Symbols, 174
Do-It-Yourself, 177
Christmas Roses, 179

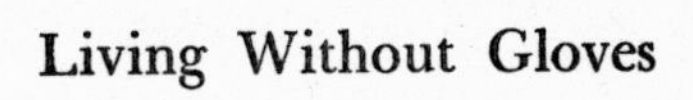
Living Without Gloves

Living Without Gloves

EDITOR, THE CHRISTIAN CENTURY:

Sir: Having learned that you are a gardener — at least, dandelions have been seen in your front yard — I am sure you will enjoy rereading, despite its strain of malice, that classic of garden poetry, "To a Fat Lady Seen from the Train," a beautiful triolet by Frances Cornford, granddaughter of Charles Darwin. Here it is:

O why do you walk through the fields in gloves,
Missing so much and so much?
O fat white woman whom nobody loves,
Why do you walk through the fields in gloves,
When the grass is soft as the breast of doves
And shivering-sweet to the touch?
O why do you walk through the fields in gloves,
Missing so much and so much?

Of course, the salute from the train is wickedly unfair. There may have been a dozen good reasons for the gloves. Perhaps it was cold. Perhaps the lady was a gardener and not a poet. Perhaps she was going out to dinner that night and didn't want "gardener's hands." But no one who has ever touched grass, "shivering-sweet," will deny that she missed a lot.

And no one can deny that a person who always handles life with gloves on, protecting him any from real contact, misses a lot. There is a very common phrase, "I handled him without gloves," which usually means: "I rushed in like a bull in a china shop, without benefit of the New Testament or even Emily Post, and let fly with both barrels." But the words can have a high meaning. "Without gloves" can denote genuine communication without barriers, the big red-letter event of life. A little picture of the frustration caused by protective gloves in human contact is found in the verses of John Nixon, Jr.:

She always wore her gloves,
The starched forbidding mesh
A barrier between
Her palm and baser flesh.

She couldn't wear her gloves
Into the Promised Land—
I wonder how she shook
St. Peter's humble hand.

"Pardon my glove" is a well-worn cliché of agonizing politeness. But life has no pardon for gloves. From the one who wraps his hand with artificial barriers to real contact it extracts the extreme penalty: missing the main show, which is always people. The glove-protected soul may take in a few of the side shows but misses the events under the big top.

As long as I have been deluging you with poetry in

this epistle, bare your head for a final spray — good advice from Grace Minard:

> *Put three fingers to the wrist of earth.*
> *Listen . . . Spring is beating fast.*

A good trick — three fingers to the wrist of life! But you can't do it with gloves, even though you are not fat and are no lady.

Yours,

SIMEON STYLITES.

Hard and Soft Saints

Sir: The business of dividing the population of the globe into two classes goes steadily on. One division I like is that which Victoria Sackville-West makes in her life of Joan of Arc. She herds the saints into two corrals, hard saints and soft saints. She has noticed, she says, that the statutes of St. Joan do not have placed before them flowers in anything like the profusion that other saints get — St. Genevieve of Paris, for example. She writes: "Not for Joan the roses and mignonette. Only the laurel and the bay. She was a hard, not a soft saint."

Of course we ought to be glad for any saints, tall or short, thick or thin, hard or soft. We have shortages of everything but shortages — certainly a grievous shortage of saints.

It is a valid distinction that Miss Sackville-West makes. And it applies to more than what my learned friends tell me is called "hagiology." It applies to all "saints" in the New Testament sense, which means the whole body of Christian disciples. The saints in Rome and Ephesus to whom Paul sent his greetings were not candidates for stained glass windows; they were the fellowship, the folks who were separated from the world and not under its domination, the whole crowd. That is where we come in.

The world has been well blessed with "soft" saints. Their hearts, thank heaven, are soft. But their heads (not so much thanks to heaven) are soft too. They are earnest, sincere, high-minded — often so high that they sail the stratosphere and rarely touch ground. There are no iron girders in their thinking. They are sentimentalists in the two senses that word has been described as having: those who "consider ends without reference to means" and those who "never follow an idea to its logical conclusion." The "hero" of Wells' *Croquet Player* was a soft saint when he said: "I am willing to fall in with any plan to save the world, but if I am asked to *think,* it is too much."

A lovely soft saint went into Franklin Simon's store in New York the other day and asked the doorman if it were Altman's. "No," said the doorman, "this is Franklin Simon's. There is the sign." "Yes," she replied plaintively, "I saw the sign, but I thought it might be Altman's." Bless her little heart! And bless her little head!

Hard saints are not so appealing and comforting as soft ones. Yet a steel girder can be a very comforting thing to people who live in a tall building. So can girders in the mind. When the sign says Franklin Simon, hard saints do not dissolve into a pipe dream thinking it might be Altman's. They look at facts and they consider means. There are many soft saints today who look out on our troubled world and cling to one romantic method of meeting all its problems: "Spend a hundred billion dollars on fireworks. That will scare 'em to death." They do not look at the fact that that, alone, has never scared anyone to death since Stone Age men first began hunting for bigger clubs. They go on thinking it might be Altman's.

Hardening of the arteries is a bad thing. But hardening of the muscles of the mind is a dependable sign of health.

Gesundheit!

SIMEON STYLITES.

Don't Cut Off the Buttons

Sir: You won't believe this, but I will swear to it on the Revised Standard Version.

One of my neighbors, a woman, like Dorcas, "full of good works," has taken vigorous part in several drives to collect clothing for Korea. She reports that on several occasions women's coats have come in with all the buttons cut off. Evidently the big-hearted, generous givers thought the buttons were quite good and could be used again, so they took the scissors and went to work, the whole gift spoiled by a nasty snip. If, as Lowell tells us, "the gift without the giver is bare," a coat without any buttons leaves the receiver very bare, too.

The moral of this mournful story is: Don't cut off the buttons! So many gifts are spoiled and soured by some little twist that keeps them from being open-hearted. So there is no kindness *de luxe* about them.

You remember the farmer's wife who asked her husband as he came in from the barn, "How much milk did the cow give?" He answered grimly, "Nine quarts and a kick." That did it. The kick knocked over the nine quarts and somewhat spoiled the total effect of the gift.

Some gifts are made with an air of patronage, a handing down from a greater height with a feeling of "Oh, did the Lord make you too?" That snips all the buttons off, no matter what the gift. Such an air in giving would make the Hope diamond look like Woolworth's second best.

A different form of cutting off the buttons, as far as the effect is concerned, is that achieved by people who call such attention to their generosity that it becomes hateful. As has been said, "When some people discharge an obligation you can hear the report for miles around."

Other gifts are like coats without buttons, they are just half done. Such half-done, slap-dash affairs are like giving your wife one earring, or giving one roller skate to a child, or passing off one glove for which you cannot find the mate, so you let it go anyhow. The extra touch with a gift, the care that says in unmistakable language, "This is a Class A event. Giving this brings me some real joy" — this is leaving the buttons on.

Many people giving to colleges and other institutions hedge the gift about with so many limitations that it is just about worthless. Like giving a college badly in the red $100,000 to erect a statue of the donor, or to endow a yearly lectureship on Patagonian wild birds.

Real adepts with the shears spoil their gifts by pouring on honeyed words, such as these that accompanied the gift of a hat by one woman to another: "My dear, I saw this lovely new hat and just couldn't resist getting it for you. We are all so tired of that ugly rag you have been wearing for five years." Snip, snip, snip go the buttons.

Compared to this shabby stuff, the Good Samaritan rated the Nobel prize for giving. He left all the buttons on his gift coat — even sent along an extra one or two, just in case. "He took out two *denarii* and gave them to the inn-keeper." He didn't measure himself out with a medicine dropper. He tossed himself about in large chunks.

Yours,

SIMEON STYLITES.

Mechanical Half-Hour

Sir: I was in the Union Station in a big city for half an hour a few weeks ago, and it was etched deep in my memory as the most mechanical half-hour in all my life. Ever since I have been wondering sort of nightmarishly whether that half-hour was a preview of a mechanical world of the future, a world so full of miraculous machines that human speech can be largely done away with, and the only thing left to shake hands with will be a push button or an occasional lever.

My first voiceless machine was the locker in which I deposited my suitcase, in which transaction the automatic lock pocketed my dime, without even a "Thank you," and handed over the key. Then I rode downstairs on an escalator (I came back on an automatic elevator). Following which I slaked my thirst with a little fountain of soda that gushed forth from a wordless machine after being thawed out with a dime. I then bought a stamp from a machine. It did not speak my language, so I could not explain that I needed only one stamp; I had to take three. Then I had my photograph taken (not from vanity, but to send it to my wife to *prove* that I hadn't left my overcoat in the train). That transaction was all mechanical and silent, except for the deep sigh I gave on looking at the exact likeness. (Sometimes it is hard to get reconciled to the will of God.) Then I had a contact in which I broke the sound barrier by one word. I pronounced the name of the town to which I wished to buy a ticket. A machine nodded "O.K." and turned out the ticket, all typed.

Seven transactions, and only one word! I began to wonder if I had died.

Then I went out on the street, stunned with loneliness in a machine world, and crossed against a red light. A big policeman saluted me warmly: "You blankety blank blank fool! The next time you do that I'll run you in!" I felt like rushing out and throwing my arms around him and crying, "Thanks, oh thanks, brother!" For that was the first kind word, or the first *word,* I had had in half an hour, the first suggestion that I was still alive and had not been changed into part of a slot machine. It was clear evidence of the truth that the worst sin against human beings is not hatred but indifference.

Is that a vision of the future, when all the brains will be mechanical and the way from the cradle to the grave will be an ingenious conveyor belt? Then the business concerns can take down the big signs saying "THINK," for it will all be done for us.

One of the unending fascinations of the Gospels is to note how Jesus kept every contact with a person from becoming mechanical. Often his friends and disciples had a way of saying "Run along!" or "Keep still!" But whenever they tried to throw up any kind of human barrier, they were reversed by higher authority. Their Master humanized every meeting.

I hope you can still say "Hi!" loud enough to be heard across the street. It is a good word, and the best noise in the world.

Yours,

SIMEON STYLITES.

"You Wouldn't Have Won If . . ."

Sir: One of Webster's cartoons that sticks in the memory pictures the end of a bridge game. A bystander is solemnly reproving the winning couple and saying, "You wouldn't have won if you had played it right."

We may smile at the unintended commentary on bridge rules. Then, when we think about it a bit longer, we realize that that remark is a profound observation on human history. You can almost elevate it to the rank of an axiom that those who have made the greatest achievements of history would not have won if they had "played it right." That is, they would not have won if they had observed all the rules of caution and prudence and made a careful calculation of probabilities. If they had done all those "right" things, they would have dropped down into little graves that had no name. Columbus did not play it right. All the wise rules of navigation were against him. (PS. He won.)

This is true not only of the high days of history but also of the low days of your own life. Your marriage, for instance. The chances are ten to one that you are one of the people who, if they had played it right, would not have got married when they did. You couldn't afford it. It was entirely against the rules, while you were getting only $1000 a year, with a good chance of getting fired next month. You were two of the millions of victims of the most beautiful lie ever invented, that "two can live as cheaply as one." You were just a couple of babes in the woods. But what lovely woods, and what wild flowers! You won!

The same is true of babies. If a couple waits until the absolutely right time to have a baby, they lose. There is no convenient time to have a baby. There never was. The greatest Baby of all was born at a very inconvenient time. The parents were on a journey. In addition to that, there was no room for them in the inn. If parents play it absolutely right, with 100 per cent caution, they never win.

If the men who fought the American Revolution had played it right they would never have won. They didn't have a sporting chance. Only a third of the people really wanted independence. The "best" people in the colonies said, "You are crazy to try to fight Great Britain with a few amateurs." They *were* crazy. So they won.

It was true of the launching of the Christian church. All the rules said, "Have a little sense. Don't rush out to the whole Roman empire unprepared. Stay here and grow quietly. Then if there seems to be a chance of success in some places, proceed prudently." They would not have grown anything except mold and rust.

It is still true. How about a plaque in the chancel with these words: "You can't win if you play it right"?

If there is to be any winning there must be risk, calculated or uncalculated. Too many churches take no chances. They say as they dig in for the duration, "A bird in the hand is worth two in the bush." That is the motto of all the cowards in the world.

There is a phrase, used by the young, expressing impatience: "Get the show on the road!" A good idea. The churches must get their "show" on the road, the greatest show on earth. Too often it is kept in winter quarters.

All aboard!

Yours,

SIMEON STYLITES.

Letter to Madison Avenue

Sir: Here is a letter I have written to a whole street, Madison Avenue, New York, the Holy Mecca of the Advertising Magicians in the United States of America. Will you please help get it delivered?

MADISON AVENUE, NEW YORK

DEAR (in a manner of speaking) STREET: I have never written to a whole street before and am at a bit of a loss. I have heard that Madison Avenue is the Royal Mile of the advertising profession, along which the Top Brains of the advertising business congregate. I hope the postman will take this letter up and down the street.

I have been listening anon and anon to the commercials on TV. I have been astounded to realize that the Top Brains of advertising, which design these commercials, do not seem to know the facts of life that are painfully evident to all viewers and hearers above the age of nine who are not in a mental institution. Your excuse is, I realize, that you live in New York and are probably out of touch with the United States of America. So here are a few facts of life about TV that have escaped you. I blush to mention them, for they are the kind of simple ideas that are disturbing to the official mind.

1. Yelling is a poor way of carrying on a conversation. Why do you have so many announcers scream their wares, like a bellowing bull caught in a barbed-wire fence? The best things in life are not accomplished by yelling. No one ever proposed to a girl by using a megaphone. Here and there an announcer talks like a man and not like a fog horn, and he is a healing poultice to the ear and mind.

2. Too much is Plenty. That is a good rule which it seems has never swung into your ken. Most of your hucksters have never heard of the "saturation point." There is one, believe me! For instance, the sadists who plan the orgy of plugging beer and cigarette commercials between every inning of a baseball game have only one rule: "Bore them to death." They argue that if one digitalis pill is good for a person with heart trouble, twenty-five pills would be a lot better. But patients have died under that regime, and many of *your* patients have disappeared.

3. A wisecrack loses its novelty after the first 10,000 times. That is heresy to the advertising Top Brass, but

remember it. When a TV listener hears for the first time that something looks good as a thingumbob should, it sounds like quite a "nifty." But after the first 10,000 times it loses its freshness. These repetitions reproduce with high fidelity the swing of a rusty gate. When we hear the witless repetition of a chain of letters such as "Ls xyz" we intone a series of our own, "Fgs su," which in the vernacular of our street means, "For goodness' sake, shut up!"

4. "Bang! Bang!" are not the only words in the English language. You have vastly overrated the appetite of the American public for murder and mayhem. Most people can get along with six murders a day or night, and with seven or eight variations of Custer's Last Stand.

An item in *Tide* a while ago stated that "quite a large volume of advertising is turning to printed media." There! Do you suppose the sponsors have been listening to TV?

Here endeth the first lesson.

As I said, will you please help get this letter delivered?

Yours,

SIMEON STYLITES.

How To Handle Your Correspondence

Sir: Realizing that one of the burdens of life which drive many people into nervous breakdowns is the matter of answering letters, I am moved to throw a rope to rescue the perishing. I know that this practical wisdom from a misspent life will be a lifesaver. Here are some things you can do with a tall pile of letters:

1. Don't do anything. Most letters will not need an answer if you give them time and don't bother them. They just automatically answer themselves. Take those letters about a crisis or several, impending in March, and "will you do something about it?" When you pick them up the 9th of May you will see that no answer is needed. They have answered themselves — one of the wonders of the age of automation, though Mr. and Mrs. Neanderthal knew about this, and besides they could use the collection of letters-on-stones to build a new hut.

2. Get some correspondence cards and a sheet of two-cent stamps. Write in a very large hand as though you were John Hancock signing the Declaration of Independence. By the time you have written "Thanks, old man" (no matter what for) and "Best wishes," there will be no more space left. That card will warm the heart of your correspondent. Two great letter writers, S. Parkes Cadman and William Lyon Phelps, practiced this art with great acclaim.

3. Answer with printed cards. I just got that tip from my insurance company. I had written them a nine-page letter explaining how I got writer's cramp and which fingers had it worst. I got a lovely printed card saying they received my letter and thank you. So I am getting some cards printed.

4. Send them your picture. You can do that with just a flip of the wrist in three seconds. The soft-minded will love it. The tough-minded have got your number already, so it will not make any difference.

5. Send the same letter in answer to all mail. This is easier on the brain cells (if any). Don't multigraph them — horrors, no! Have your wife, poor wretch (as Pepys used to refer to his beloved), do the typing. All you need to do is to put in the address. Have her explain that you have a severe case of enocholotis. That does not mean anything but is impressive. Have her say it is not fatal but will incapacitate you for two months. Meanwhile you can live happily ever after.

6. Finally — *and this is important:* If you get a letter from the Village Improvement Society of Horseheads, New York, asking you to speak for half an hour on "The Past, Present and Future of Civilization," for twenty-five dollars, *Don't Write — Telegraph.* Telegraph (collect) the word "Yes!"

Hoping to hear from you,

Yours,

SIMEON STYLITES.

"She'll Be Comin' Round the Mountain"

Sir: A crowd of youngsters in a church parlor were having a Christmas "sing" around a briskly burning fire on the hearth. One lad with a lovely whisky tenor started the old song "She'll be comin' round the mountain when she comes." The leader — in this case a "leaderess" — was shocked. "No, no!" she cried. "That is *not* a Christmas carol." And all melody stopped short.

But one observer, all set to burst into barbershop chords, said to himself: "You're all wrong, sister! That emphatically *is* a Christmas carol, and a good one." For "she'll be comin' round the mountain when she comes" is a forecast of hope, in a world where hope is in very short supply. It is the business of Christmas to bring hope. It began that way — "to give light to them that sit in darkness and in the shadow of death." And that is right where we sit today, "in the shadow of death."

We are in a mountain country. If there is to be any real hope for the world, think of the mountains we must get around. Mountains of prejudice that loom like Everest, mountains of ignorance, of ancestral blindness, of entrenched privilege, of inertia, which block the road to a better world like a range of the Rockies.

So the news that "she'll be comin' round the mountain" is "good news which shall be to all people." This is not only hope; it is history. For a "great day coming" *has* come around great mountains. Think of the power of the slave trade in England in the eighteenth century. *There* was a mountain that sat on top of trade, of government and, yes, of the church. But change did come around it.

We read in the letter to the Corinthians of "faith to remove mountains." But if the mountains of evil don't move — and a lot of them seem to be set pretty solidly — we can come around them. There are mountains that we cannot blast away or tunnel through. Christmas hope and faith sings that "she'll be comin' round the mountains" that block the way.

Thus, Christmas saves us from the ultimate despair, such as that of the dying H. G. Wells, who wrote in his last years: "It now seems to me that the whole universe is utterly bored by the whole species of mankind. I can see the human race sweeping along the stream of fate to defeat, degradation and final defeat." That seems to cover it! No program ahead except that of Richard II:

For God's sake, let us sit upon the ground
And tell sad stories of the death of kings.

There is another line of action. We can all rise and instead of intoning that dirge we can sing a different tune: "He shall reign forever and ever."

We are told that Christmas is this and Christmas is that. As a matter of fact Christmas is a whistle, proclaiming that something is coming round the mountain. It may be away off, but she'll be comin', sure. So get up on tiptoe and listen. Can't you hear it? There it is: "The dayspring from on high hath visted us . . . And thou, Child, shalt go before the face of the Lord to prepare his ways, and . . . guide our feet into the way of peace."

So deck the halls with holly!

Yours,

SIMEON STYLITES.

Performing Lion

Sir: Listen to a short poem — short, but it starts long, long thoughts. It is by that Irish magician with words Lord Dunsany, in the *Saturday Evening Post* not so long ago, entitled "Dirge for a Performing Lion." There is a wonderful legerdemain with language, portraying the King of Beasts as he was in Africa, with muscles able and ready to "leap as swift as a waterfall," eyes to peer through the jungle darkness, and a "mane of splendor." He has memories of Africa, where he "walked in the morning light like a king in gold." And then comes the crushing anticlimax: "He sits upon a barrel and drinks tea."

It is a picture for the imagination. But it is hard to keep one's thoughts from making an unscheduled detour from the subject of a captured lion to the subject of the church. This might be a good poem to put on the church calendar. Perhaps it would rank in importance with the announcement that Circle C of the Women's Society will have a tea Thursday at three p.m.

For like the lion on a barrel drinking tea, the church

can revolve old memories, of the day when it "walked in the morning light like a king in gold" and the startled bystanders exclaimed, "These men who have turned the world upside down have come here also!" The church too had sinews able to make a sudden leap at evil. It could confront the powers of earth with an unterrified "We must obey God rather than man." Thank heaven, the church still has sinews to leap into battle in God's holy war. The daring protests against racial injustice in South Africa by Michael Scott and Trevor Huddleston and others stir the blood.

But that only makes the more dismal the shabby anticlimax, when a church with these "bright memories" "sits upon a barrel and drinks tea." That picture brings to mind the recent comment of Leslie Weatherhead that "far too much Christianity is floated on afternoon tea parties." It does not always float; sometimes it sinks and drowns in oolong.

Benjamin Franklin once used aptly this metaphor of a forcibly tamed lion, when his "nice-Nellie" grandson toned down his autobiography because he thought the language not cultured enough. The angry Benjamin said: "He has drawn the teeth and pared the nails of my paper, so that it can neither scratch nor bite. It can only paw and mumble." Sometimes the gospel is mumbled.

Wouldn't it be exciting if the lion on a barrel drinking tea should really revive its golden memories and leap up from the barrel? In Section III of the report of the World Council of Churches' Evanston assembly we find these words: "In all these fields the real dangers are complacency, lack of imagination, and the dull sense of hopelessness that settles upon those of little faith." That is just what we were saying, in other words: the greatest dangers to the church are a barrel and a cup of tea.

How about starting the leap? One, two, three!

Yours,

SIMEON STYLITES.

"I Remember, I Remember"

Sir: Out on the front porch the other night the conversation began to show unmistakable signs of expiring, giving little despairing gasps, like an automobile running out of gas. But before it actually gave up the ghost a quick-witted neighbor, who had taken a Red Cross first-aid course, rushed in with an oxygen tank and restored life. She did it by asking this question: "What sounds or odors made the sharpest impression on you as a child? What do you remember with the deepest intensity?" With that all the folks came out of their coma and perked up. (Try it some time. In fact, you might do it yourself right now.)

Here are a few things from Memory Lane, as the company on the porch rushed down it: the creak of wagon wheels on a zero morning, as heard by a child in bed; the grinding sound of a coffee mill that came up from the kitchen early in the morning; the tinkle of an alarm clock, like the crack of doom, which it was; the distant sound of a railroad engine whistle, two long blasts and three short ones (what a loss that lovely sound is, and what a feeble substitute is the ugly growl of a Diesel engine!); the barking of a hound dog; the lowing of cattle waiting at the meadow fence to be brought home at night.

And a few fragrances — two that would appear high on any poll: the smell of wood smoke and burning leaves; the smell of coffee in the drawer of the coffee mill, where the fragrance of a thousand teaspoonfuls of coffee had permeated the very wood (what a feeble substitute any tin can is for that!). The licorice in an old-fashioned "jawbreaker"!

I noticed lately that Van Wyck Brooks has been playing the same game, and here are some memories he came up with: "The winding of the clock on Sunday morning; the mowing of the lawn and the far-away beating of carpets; the whirring of water sprinklers and the rocking of hammocks."

The game wasn't all wasted time. One conclusion reached was, "Stop, Look, and Listen" more carefully to the pageant of life as it rolls by. Thus, we might have more bright points of light in the memory. We go down the roads with a worried look and blind eyes and deaf ears.

A violet by the river's brim
Is very commonplace and dim.

Audrey Wurdemann, the poet, has conjured up an alluring bit of fancy:

To see
With the eye of a fly

Or with the furred ear of a deer
To hear what no others can hear.

That would be an exquisite heightening of the senses. We could not stand it. But we can, if we wish, come a lot nearer to it than we do. Life need not be the blindman's buff that we make it.

Give me not scenes more charming,
Give me eyes.

What sounds or odors made the sharpest dent on your recollection?

Yours,

SIMEON STYLITES.

"London Grace"

Sir: "London grace" is a special kind of grace not mentioned in the New Testament. But it is a handy kind to have around. It was John Newton of Olney, England, who once made a fervent prayer for "London grace." He thus explained it: "By London grace I mean grace in a very high degree, grace to enable one to live as a Christian even in London."

John Newton knew a good deal about grace. His life was fantastic beyond belief. If a fictionalized version of it were submitted to a publisher it would be turned down as being so utterly far from probability that the public would not swallow it. The public never swallows a lot that is done by the grace of God! Newton ran away to sea, was sold as a slave, became captain of a slave ship, then a clergyman at Olney (where he was the intimate friend of the poet Cowper) and the author of such deathless hymns as "Glorious Things of Thee are Spoken" and "How Sweet the Name of Jesus Sounds." When he went to be the vicar of a London church he felt the need of London grace.

Is there a special kind of grace that will enable a person to survive spiritually in a large city? Any New York grace? Or Chicago grace? That *would* be miraculous grace! Still, there were saints in Caesar's household and there are saints in Chicago. Honest! I know some of them.

At this point someone will rise and say that it doesn't take any more grace to live decently in Chicago or Los Angeles than it does to live in the country; that the old slander that "God made the country and the devil made the town" was blown up long ago. All right. But city life still needs a kind of "London grace." We need physical grace to dodge cars. It's as bad as sliding for second base, and you don't have a uniform on either.

Abundant grace is needed to withstand the compulsion of mass stimulation. The city world is so full of a number of things that we are stimulated in six directions at once, and are shaped accordingly, processed by pressurizing. It is strange that the sharpest description of this hazard should come from the African jungle, from Dr. Schweitzer:

> The man of today is exposed to influences which are bent on robbing him of all confidence in his own thinking. The spirit of spiritual dependence to which he is called on to surrender is in everything he hears and reads. It is in everyone he meets . . . and in all the circumstances of his life.

A related danger is that of being robbed of individuality by the crowd mentality. It is as hard to find a spot for solitude as to find a place to park a car. Solitude goes out of life and the plural world rushes in. Robert L. Linder, writing about urban youth, describes a threat to all who live amid the canyons and cliffs of a city: "Youth today has abandoned solitude for pack-running, for predatory assembly, for great collectivities that bury, if they do not destroy, individuality . . . The fee they pay for initiation is abandonment of self and immersion in the herd."

In the inevitable anonymous quality of city life there is the risk of becoming callous. If the milkman who delivers to your apartment slips and breaks his hip, the best you can summon is a more or less casual "Tough break." But in the country or small town you would know him and would have your feelings lacerated. It is less of a strain on the feelings to live in a city — and much more of a danger of the atrophy of sympathy and the onset of galloping callousness.

Will you please write a Collect for Those in Perils of Cities?

Yours,

SIMEON STYLITES.

No Time for Barak

Sir: This is a little story about a man who never got a break. He appears (and very briefly, too) in Hebrews 11:32: ". . . time would fail me to tell of Gideon, Barak, Samson, David . . ." See what I mean? No time for Barak. There has been plenty of time to speak of Gideon and Samson and David. Only Barak has passed into oblivion, for lack of time. Flimsy excuse! Gideon and Samson have had their public relations people working overtime. Not all the hosts of N.B.C. and C.B.S. could have done a better job. Gideon appears in every hotel room in America. Samson is known the world over as the first holder of the World's Championship Belt, long before John L. Sullivan came along. Samson also gets credit for a great invention, a weapon still used in war and political campaigns: the jawbone of an ass. David is well advertised. Every second boy is named David. But who ever heard of a Barak W. Jones?

Time fails to speak of Barak. It isn't fair. For Barak was a stout lad. He overthrew the armies of Sisera in mortal combat, but in spite of all his valor "time fails." Barak composed a famous song with Deborah, but who grabbed off the credit? Why Deborah, of course. Never trust a woman! It says plainly in Judges 5:1, "Then sang Deborah *and Barak*." Half the copyright belongs to Barak; but it is known the world over as "Deborah's Song." Again a shabby trick of fame. "Time failed" to tell of Barak.

The Baraks of this world are a large tribe. They are the people who really do a job, but they never take a bow, for time fails to mention them; they plod along anonymously. The Baraks smite the Siseras, but there is no time to speak of them. In a church, Barak often carries the load; he fixes the roof; he holds off the sheriff with a shotgun; he teaches the boys' class that ought to be called "Juvenile Delinquents, Inc." Mrs. Barak — girl and woman — served up dinners enough to feed the children of Israel forty years in the wilderness without any help from manna, either. The beans had to be baked. But when the Anniversary Celebration comes around and the gold medals are hung on swelling breasts, are the Baraks in the front row? Don't be foolish! Time fails to speak of the Baraks. They are still taken for granted, as they have been through the ages.

So in biography. When the pageant of the great is unfolded, you can be sure that somewhere concealed is a Barak who played a major role. But time failed to hint of him. Yet the unpublicized Baraks are often the real *doers*. They deserve the tribute paid to Joseph: "Whatever they did there, he was the doer of it." Who wrote "Adeste Fideles"? Why, Barak, of course! Anonymously. Who invented the wheel? Ten to one it was a Barak, unspoken of by a fickle fame, a *doing* Barak for whom time failed.

Still, there is a lot more fun being a Barak and doing a job than being a graven image who is getting the citation. And Barak brings to mind a nice little idea about eternity. There will be plenty of time there to pick up some odds and ends for which "time failed" down here. Over there, time will not fail to mention Barak. There will be plenty of time to speak of him, and that will be a story worth listening to. Get your reservations for that stirring revelation.

Yours,

SIMEON STYLITES.

TV and the Canadian Rockies

Sir: A news item announced that the Canadian National Railways have equipped their transcontinental trains with television. This is set forth as a lure to travel. I doubt its pulling power. Perhaps some of the customers might be running away from TV!

But this announcement is surely a symbol of a disease which afflicts many in this generation, that of taking things at second hand instead of first-hand participation. We seem, many of us, to have progressively less and less capacity to enjoy and profit by first-hand experience.

Just drop the picture into your imagination. The

coast-to-coast supertrain is going through the Canadian Rockies, passing some of the most marvelous scenery in the world, breath-taking beauty and grandeur which brings awe to the mind and spirit. But, instead of looking at these wonders of the world, you can sit inside a darkened car and gape open-mouthed at Howdy Doody or Milton Berle or a soap opera which is a direct descendant of the old "Perils of Pauline." Isn't science wonderful?

Thus, we have an example of what has been called a "disease of modern civilization," a disease which surfeits men and women with artificial entertainment and makes them unable to draw satisfaction from any natural source or from within themselves. If you cease to entertain them, they wither.

Second-hand living inevitably makes second-rate people.

In political life so many hundreds of thousands of people have no first-hand participation, no contact with the real thing at all. All they have is a second- or third-hand impression from the newspapers. And in most cases these are a marvelous medium for seeing through a glass darkly.

In the field of sports we are becoming no longer even spectators. Instead of going out to the ball park where you can have a spiritual workout by yelling for the home team and cursing the umpire, we stay at home and see some of it on a little screen. Fifty or even forty years ago a baseball game was the leading feature of the Sunday school picnic. Today it would be hard to find a dozen men who have caught a baseball in twenty years.

And for that matter, where can you find a Sunday school picnic? That was a thrilling first-hand contact with nature with ants in the sandwiches, and the grounds beautifully decorated with a thick border of poison ivy! Instead we are likely to have something served up by the Audio-Visual Committee.

This fatal living at second hand can work devastation in religion. We have many a learned discussion of religion by people who have never had any religious experience at all. Chesterton put it well when he described how the wild surmise came into his mind that "perhaps those might not be the best judges of the relation of religion and happiness who, by their own confession, had never experienced either!"

Why not turn off the TV and look at the Rockies?

Yours,

SIMEON STYLITES.

"We'll Be So Respectable—"

Sir: The mother of G. K. Chesterton once made a remark in the bosom of her family which seems to me to deserve resurrection in each new generation. It was on the occasion when her husband, Edward Chesterton, received recognition of his ability and growing influence by being elected to the vestry of the Anglican church in the village. He brought the good news home to his wife, but she was appalled. "Don't take it," she pleaded. "Oh, Edward, we'll be so respectable. We've never been respectable. Let's not begin now."

I enclose one dollar to start a fund for inscribing those words on tablets to be placed in the vestibules of churches. For I can detect a distinct New Testament flavor to the words. "We've never been respectable" is an echo across the years of other words, "Not many wise, not many noble," in St. Paul's description of the Christian company.

Of course, Mrs. Chesterton was using the word "respectable" in its peculiar nineteenth-century sense, with its prim correctness. The figures of Albert the Good and his wife, Queen Victoria, rigidly formidable in black silk bombazine, hover around the edges of the word. Jane Austen's novels are a voluminous commentary on it.

Mrs. Chesterton had seen many vestrymen, and had a terrifying vision of her warmly human husband on his way to become one of Mrs. Jarley's Wax Works, attired in funereal garb of high silk hat, Prince Albert coat, striped trousers, and decorous gloves. To all that her soul cried out, "Let's not begin now!"

Of course, there is a high meaning to the word, "respectable." It can denote reverence for a great tradition. But, in common use, it travels on a much lower level, described in the dictionary as "respect for proprieties, conventionally correct in conduct." It becomes an undue concern for irrelevant standards.

In its great hours, Christianity has never been "respectable." It was one of the deadly charges against Jesus that he was the friend of sinners and ate with publicans and other riffraff. How "respectable" were John Bunyan and George Fox? Or the great unwashed who were the first converts of the evangelical revival in the eighteenth century?

Like the Byzantine church, some churches have become a sort of court religion of complacent security. Respectability stands high on any valid list of the Seven Deadly Virtues. When we become whaleboned in a conventional, prudential stiffness, we trade a sense of mission to the last, the least, and the lost for a keen sense of protective coloration. Then *rigor mortis* sets in.

An honest death notice might well be:

> DIED, November 1957, Grace Church, of Megapolis, U.S.A., aged 100 years, of acute respectability, resulting in hardening of the spiritual arteries.

Yours,

SIMEON STYLITES.

Render Unto Caesar

Sir: What would you say is the devil's favorite text from the Bible? Perhaps you think the devil does not read the Bible. Wrong again! We have it on the revered authority of Shakespeare in *The Merchant of*

Venice that "the devil can cite scripture for his purpose." More than that, we have all heard him quoting piously many Bible verses. The devil's favorite texts surely must be those that can be deftly twisted to befuddle people. One of the best pictures of the devil cleverly at work is Kipling's

> *to hear the truth you've spoken*
> *Twisted by knaves to make a trap for fools.*

High among the devil's preferences in Holy Writ must be the verses that can be perversely warped out of their real meaning to make nice booby traps. Here is a beauty: "For you always have the poor with you." That has been continuously twisted by knaves to induce the belief that the evil of poverty is set in the world as permanently as gravitation.

Another honey, lifted out of its context and distorted, is, "I have not come to bring peace, but a sword." And the devil whispers behind the leaves of the Book, "There is your blessing on war."

Another good one is, "Let your moderation be known to all men." The devil gets many folks to take that as their motto, many of them pulpit spellbinders, and they let their moderation be known — immoderately!

But the devil's first choice certainly must be, "Render unto Caesar the things that are Caesar's and unto God the things that are God's." What could be more reasonable? The catch lies in dividing the "things." It develops that nearly everything that matters much is claimed by Caesar, and the leftovers for God are pretty slim.

Increasingly, Caesar, in the form of large business concerns, takes over everything from the up-and-coming executive, even to the kind of car he drives, the clothes his wife wears, and his opinions on every subject except geometry.

Caesar, as the government, increasingly says, "Your ideas are mine to determine. If you think anything except the least common denominator of conformity, you are out of line. Your conscience is my affair. I will take over your thinking on war and foreign policy. Better come along quietly." A reasonable text, "Render unto God the things that are God's" — if you can discover anything that Caesar has overlooked!

Lewis Carroll has drawn the classic and well-nigh perfect picture of Caesar in action. The Owl and the Panther dine together (Caesar is the Panther):

I passed by his garden and marked with one eye
How the Owl and the Panther were sharing a pie;
The Panther took pie-crust, and gravy, and meat,
While the Owl had the dish as its share of the treat.
When the pie was all finished, the Owl, as a boon,
Was kindly permitted to pocket the spoon;
While the Panther received knife and fork with a growl
And concluded the banquet — by eating the Owl!

Yours,

SIMEON STYLITES.

He Ate with the Crew

Sir: Once upon a time, in fact it was six months ago (this is my true story), a man signed up for a cruise of a few months on a swanky cruise ship. There was a hoity-toity crowd of passengers, with plenty of glitter and glare, right out of the Social Register and Dun & Bradstreet. They were devotees of pleasure, determined to have a good time if it killed them. Every evening there was a sound of revelry by night, and in the daytime there was quite a continuous obbligato produced by the clinking of glassware. This man, after a few days of voyaging on that sea of cocktails, thought of Lord Byron's division of the human race:

Society is now one polish'd horde,
Formed of two mighty tribes, the Bores *and* Bored.

The only difference was that on this cruise the two tribes were the same.

Our voyager made a discovery that sounded like old-hat Sunday school stuff: that the people whose one aim is pleasure pay a terrible price. They get to be the most tiresome bores on earth. They get out of touch with the world of workers. They do not have either toughened hands or toughened brains. As daily companions, they add up pretty close to zero.

So this man wandered down to the quarters of the crew and found it quite a different dish. Here were real people; they did not have to bluff or put on either "front" or "side." They could indulge in the luxury of being themselves. And they were infinitely more interesting than the "quality" on Deck A. They worked for a living and had something to report. Our voyager spent all his time with them, ate with them, and had a real cruise in human nature. It was of course an old discovery — that people who work for a living are a lot better company than the poor drudges who have to spend their time trying to run away from themselves. Rudyard Kipling made the same discovery on his world cruise in 1881. He records that he spent most of his time "with the crew in pajamas, sitting abaft the funnel, swapping lies."

The pursuit of pleasure gets to be a dull game. That sounds like a copybook maxim, but the funny thing about copybook maxims is that sometimes they are true.

Back in the 1920's a critic made a pertinent comment on an assemblage of pleasure hounds, those pictured in Ernest Hemingway's *The Sun Also Rises.* That book has the longest barroom in the world, stretching from the English Channel to the Pyrenees. The critic wrote:

> It is the great moral tract of the age. It will drive all the amateur reprobates in the English-speaking world to cold showers and bran muffins . . . No one can stand a continuous round of monotonous gaiety forever. You feel that these creatures really have a nice hectic game of croquet coming to them, just to put a little color

in their drab lives. They may be bad eggs, but surely God never meant the least of his creatures to be so bored.

The late lamented David Roberts summed it up. "When we try to reach happiness on cheap terms," he said, "what we get is bound to be cheap. That is why pleasure seekers in any age are always the most bored and dissatisfied people on earth. That is why anyone who aims directly as self-realization turns out to be only a fraction of a man." *

Since we have been handing out Sunday school stuff, let's make it a day and sing "Work for the Night is Coming," No. 149 in the little red book.

Yours,

SIMEON STYLITES.

Jumping Out of Your Skin

Sir: A few days ago a man in a crowded street walked up behind another man and suddenly laid a hand on his shoulder. The man who was laid hold on gave a start and said, "You made me jump out of my skin." "That might be a good idea," said the first man.

That is a trivial conversation to be reported in these august pages. Yet it has a lot of the past, present, and future of civilization in it. Jumping out of your skin is the top athletic achievement of the human race. It

* From *The Grandeur and Misery of Man,* Oxford University Press, New York.

is the High Jump and the Broad Jump combined, and some notable records have been made in the event. It means jumping out of your skin into another person's, so that you can feel where the burdens of life rest heavily on him and cut cruelly into him. We are too skin-bound, too enclosed by the narrow limits of circumscribed experience.

Here is a man who was not adept at jumping out of his skin — Lord Curzon, "the Exquisite." While inspecting British troops in France during the First World War he watched the soldiers taking shower baths. He exclaimed in amazement, "It is remarkable what white skins the lower orders have." He probably thought — if he ever thought about it at all — that the "lower orders" or working people in London, Manchester, and Birmingham had black or red skins, marking them off from the aristocracy. He never jumped out of his own skin to see. That is the cardinal sin of class blindness.

One of the best things that could happen in the world would be for more and more people to go in for athletics and specialize in jumping out of their skin. For the next score of years the United States will be engaged in that kind of jump, followed the lead of the Supreme Court — the jump out of white skin into skin of darker color, endeavoring to understand the experience of Negroes and other groups under segregation and discrimination.

In the larger Field Day, that of international relations, there will have to be a lot of skin-jumping. The hatred of much of Asia for the West comes largely from a century of failure on the part of white men to change their skin, to feel how the yellow men of China and Japan and the brown men of India feel. The East is not having any more of the white man's flaunting "superiority." It has had enough. The present convulsion in Asia is partly the result of a century's resentment of it. This is vividly pictured in the words of Justice William O. Douglas of the Supreme Court: "We of the West have gone to these other continents harshly, arrogantly and oppressively. Our attitudes have been haughty and overbearing. From the earliest days our emissaries have been freebooters and buccaneers of one kind and another." In other words, we did not jump out of our skin.

Walt Whitman wrote of his work with wounded soldiers in the hospitals of Washington during the Civil War: "I do not give jelly and fruit to the wounded man. I *become* the wounded man myself." There is probably some of Walt's melodramatics in that. But it is a good idea.

On your marks! Get set!

Yours,

SIMEON STYLITES.

Books for Tired Eyes

Sir: The American Library Association has in stock a pamphlet which ought to bring joy to a large number of people. It is entitled *Books for Tired Eyes,* a list of books for varying tastes, fiction and nonfiction, that are printed in 12-point type or larger. It ought to prove a new gateway to the joys of reading for those with impaired sight or with "tired eyes."

In that connection, it is worth recording that the Devil's crowning masterpiece is the type in which most Bibles are printed. If there is a better way of making void the word of God no one has discovered it. There must be millions of children who have received presents of a Bible printed in type so small that it might as well be Hindustani.

But I have got off the track. This started out to be a different kind of wail. My eyes are very tired from looking at many books — some of them at the top of the best-seller lists — and trying to read them. Very, very tired.

My eyes are tired of books by John O'Hara and Erskine Caldwell and other geniuses of the Bawdy School of fiction. I prefer to take my Jukeses and Kallikaks straight, as serious discussions of social problems, and not served up with alleged humor as obscene jokes. I prefer sex straight, as in the Kinsey report, instead of beaten up into a novel.

I write not as a moralist, but as a reader of fiction. For if it is true that all work and no play makes Jack a dull boy, then all sex and no love makes him a much duller boy, and makes Jill a figure of no more interest than a recurring decimal.

It is, of course, true that sin has been a tremendous

theme for great fiction and drama. But it is the background of a sense of an august moral law that is being violated which gives meaning to the novel or drama. It has been pertinently observed that if a fall from virtue has no more significance than a stumble at the curbstone, the record of twenty-two stumbles in 567 pages can be as dull as a city directory.

My eyes are tired of synthetic historical novels, all with the same flaming jacket featuring the same anatomy. Most of them are a cut above *Forever Amber,* but of the same general type, recording things the likes of which never were on land or sea. We have the building of the Pyramids with a close-up of Gloriana pursued by a troop of lovers; the Battle of Waterloo with a close-up of Gloriana pursued by a regiment of lovers, including Wellington and Napoleon; the Gold Rush to California with a close-up of Gloriana pursued by the same pack, this time in Wild West costumes. After a dozen of them in one season, you begin to get, in a rough way, a general idea of how it goes.

My eyes are tired of books of alleged psychology, books on "How to Emerge from the Washtub and Become a Queen of the Ballroom in Four Easy Lessons." There is a vigorous American illusion that the answer to anything can be found in a book somewhere. One of our big industries is capitalizing on the national inferiority complex and on envy and greed deliberately stirred up.

My eyes are more tired still when religion is dragged in by so-called religious books, presenting religion as a means, always a means, of getting something else. "You too, can be a Big Booming Success, with the help of Religion. Religion will enable you to master worry, bunions, shyness, pimples, dollar shortage, or what have you."

So I am glad there are books for tired eyes to turn to. Call me an old fogy or a refugee from the Victorian Age. I don't care so long as I can rest my eyes with Jane Austen, Dickens, Conrad, Dostoevski, and Melville, with Willa Cather and Ellen Glasglow, with John Buchan and A. Conan Doyle, and with a score of living writers.

There is another book I have heard of, a sort of memoirs of a physician. Luke is the name, I think. Can you tell me where I can get a copy?

Yours,

SIMEON STYLITES.

Whooping Crane

Sir: As of this moment, my favorite animal is the Whooping Crane. More power to his scrawny wings and louder whoops to his husky throat! His valiant battle against the extinction of his species has a large crowd of spectators goggle-eyed with suspense. We are told that there are only thirty-two whooping cranes known to be in existence, plus those hopes for the future, two new eggs. Will they escape going the way of the dodo and the dinosaur? I never saw a whooping crane, I never hope to see one, but it will be sad to hear the last whoop.

It occurs to a weak, impressionable mind that there are other valuable species among the fauna of American life which look to be near extinction. So I am organizing a Society for the Preservation of Rare Animals.

One variety of family which, like the whooping crane, seems to be passing away is the family that bought books. There are, thank heaven, more than thirty-two of them still alive. But they seem to be disappearing. Remember when people bought books? Books were standard equipment for a home. The family did not have a power lawnmower, except for Dad and the kids, or a washing machine, except for Mom, but they had *books* and paid real money for them. Builders report that they are putting up a rapidly decreasing number of houses with bookcases. Bookcases are getting to be as obsolete as a churn in the home. And even where there are bookcases they are often filled with china dogs and other cultural gadgets. Save the book buyers, for they are the hope of any tomorrow worth sticking around for.

Another vanishing species seems to be the home where the kids practiced music lessons and learned to play with their own hands. Of course some of these are left, as there are some of the whoopers. Perhaps I don't hear them because I live in the cultural slums. Let's try to save the species.

Still another disappearing animal is that known in

other days as a "character." The word did not describe an "eccentric" or a "nitwit" but a person of strong, colorful individuality. "Characters" are sadly missed these days when so many of the populace seem to be cut out with the same biscuit cutter, all the same size, all with the same taste (that of unsalted dough). "Characters" followed the pattern of that patron saint of New England Henry David Thoreau, who, when asked at about the age of eight what he was going to be, replied laconically, "I'll be I." (He *was!*) Today the standard answer seems to be, "I'll be everybody else." Alas, in many places today individualists like Thoreau, who enrich the common life, would be arrested for the monstrous crime of deviation from the accepted pattern.

At any rate, don't shoot! Save the species!

Yours,

SIMEON STYLITES.

In Defense of Gossip

Sir: When Robert Louis Stevenson was in his lonely exile in San Francisco, skirting the edge of death from tuberculosis, he wrote to a friend back home in Scotland, "Why does everyone send me sermons? Why doesn't someone send me gossip that I am dying for?"

In that reproachful question Stevenson was speaking for the human race. There are many times when our spiritual constitution needs good gossip more than sermons. For news is usually a better boon than advice. There are times when we feel strongly, "And now abideth faith, hope and love, and the greatest of these is gossip." There is often a saving power in gossip — the power of saving life from extinction by abstraction. There are many times when our mind turns eagerly, not to the spiritual issues of civilization, but to the question, "What on earth are the Joneses going to do next?"

Of course, gossip has a bad name, because so much malice is associated with gossip. There is no defense for vicious, mean-spirited talk. The Apostle James handled that issue for all time. There is no defense for a tongue like Jane Welsh Carlyle's, which was, someone reported, "like a cat's, which would take the skin off at a touch." Perhaps that kindly remark was just an example of vicious malice — though it must be admitted that most of us relish a bit of benign malice, such as that in the classic tribute to George Grote, the historian, and his wife. Someone, possibly Sydney Smith, said, "I like the Grotes. George is so sweet, and Mrs. Grote is such a manly fellow." That is not poison; it is just a wallop in good clean fun.

But gossip, in the true and undefiled sense, is nourishment from the good earth of the doings of people. Christian love and gossip stem from the same root: an interest in other people. When that interest is lacking much of the saving salt of life is gone. Thoreau wrote one thing in *Walden* that is colossally wrong, except as a personal confession. He said: "For my part I could easily do without the post office. I think there are very few important communications made through it. To speak critically, I never received more than one or two letters in my life that were worth the postage." Such a petition in bankruptcy excites only pity in anyone who has ever enjoyed the luxury of devouring a vivacious, newsy, gossipy letter. A missive like that is worth far more than the postage. It is water to a thirsty soul, good news from a far country. Life takes a sharp revenge on such disdain for small human happenings. Part of the price to Thoreau was that he was exiled from the joys of easy friendship, as shown in Emerson's remark that he would as soon think of taking the arm of an elm tree as Thoreau's. Thoreau wrote, "I wanted to drive life into a corner and reduce it to its lowest terms." But if life driven into a corner is robbed of a continuing interest in the folks around us, then the terms are far too low for human nature's daily food.

We would seriously question the reality of "love of humanity" in anyone who did not have stirred into it a lively interest in good gossip.

Oh, yes, I almost forgot. What is the news down your way?

Yours,

SIMEON STYLITES.

New Look in Preachers' Wives

Sir: This seems to be the season for changing models. All the new automobiles for 1956 are heralded as "revolutionary." But they all look like automobiles to me, with four wheels and a trunk. The most radical changes are in the marked-up prices.

But I do notice real change in models in another field of national interest, that of Ministers' Wives. There is something real going on there, visible to the naked eye. There is a new freedom for the minister's wife to revolt from being a type and to become an individual. The old model, so widely produced, where the poor girl was a slave to a preconceived idea of what a preacher's wife ought to be, is being rapidly retired. She used to be shown one model and told that she had better conform—or else. Lincoln freed the slaves, and time and good sense are bringing freedom to the preacher's wife to be herself.

Look at some of the ancient models that are passing out of production and becoming, by the grace of God, obsolete.

1. *The Solemn Saint.* This was a widely distributed model. Don't get me wrong. I'm all for saints. But not professional saints, not saints by compulsion, which the woman in the manse often was. I like my saints like St. Theresa, with a sense of humor and a fiery temper. She made a prayer that has come down to us: "From sullen saints, good Lord, deliver us." The ladies of the congregation often thought the preacher's wife should be a disembodied spirit whose greatest thrill was to play the piano in prayer meeting.

2. *The Wifely Pastor's Assistant.* This model was very popular with those in the congregation who liked the Giant Economy Size, getting two workers for one salary. This model is still in production, but the de-

mand is slackening. There are still some preachers' wives who fall in with this demand, and feel that they bring the greatest joy to their husbands by being "right in there pitching all the time." Perhaps the poor man might like to do the pitching himself, or get off the diamond altogether and go to the movies, instead of discussing for the nth time the crisis in the cradle roll.

3. *The Protecting Mother Model.* There was large production in this, but it too has fallen off. This model was devoted to keeping her Beloved from taking any risk, sheltering him from all danger and undue exertion. The bride grows into a "put-on-your-rubbers" girl. She cautions, "Must you always climb out on a limb? It's a lot safer back near the trunk." Edward A. Steiner has drawn her picture:

> A wife wants to mother her darling prophet and keep him from harm, and she often smothers his prophetic eloquence, for is he not hers? She acts protectively and manages to slip a silken B.V.D. shirt under the hair shirt he tries to wear, and a velvet cushion under the crown of thorns. Thus she can turn whatever bark he has into the whine of a Pekingese.

The big change has been from model into individual and from "lady" into woman. Just a caution: Stand fast in the freedom which you have been given.

Yours,

SIMEON STYLITES.

Will You Marry Me?

Sir: In this heyday of anthologies someone, sooner or later, will get up an anthology of proposals of marriage, representing all the varied temperatures of man's heart and mind. They will range all the way from the lyric and ecstatic to the subzero emotion of the man who led his intended to the family lot in the cemetery and asked her how she would like to lie there, eventually.

We offer for the low temperature prize the letter in which Edward Dickinson, father of Emily Dickinson, proposed marriage to his future wife. He wrote:

> Let us prepare for a life of rational happiness. I do not either wish or expect a life of pleasure. May we be happy and useful and successful and each be an ornament in society, and gain the respect and confidence of all with whom we may be connected.

What a delirious program! Nothing incendiary there! He had a firm grip on himself. We can measure some of the world's progress, particularly woman's progress, by the fact that hardly any girl in the nation would today say "Yes" to such a sensible offer. She would say, "No, thank you! I do not want to be an ornament. You go over and perch on the what-not and be an ornament all by yourself. I'd rather marry a hot-headed lad foolish enough to love me."

This letter does have a mournful suggestion in another realm than that of marriage. It represents the exact emotional temperature and excitement of many people in regard to religion and the church. Austerely rational, everything under control. No danger of forgetting themselves in any indiscretion of generosity. No silly nonsense like finding their life by losing it.

When passion glows, with heat intense,
They turn the hose of common sense
And out it goes, with small expense.

The greatest enemy of love is common sense, as frequently defined. The greatest enemy of Christianity is common sense. The two people to whom Jesus gave the most lyrical praise, the woman who anointed him with costly perfume and the woman who put all her living into the alms box, were eminently foolish. They let themselves go, unchecked by common sense which would whisper, "Go easy, sister."

Many years ago a young man in Pittsburgh was courting (that was the expression then) a girl who lived out on Herron hill, at the end of the carline to the east. For two years he went out to see her every Wednesday night. Finally he asked her to marry him. She refused, and he was dumfounded. She explained her refusal thus: "For two years you have been out here every Wednesday night. Never once did you miss the last car back to the city. I can't risk a man who never forgets himself." Bright girl!

A church in which the emotional temperature is set by the Edward Dickinsons will never

> *Climb the steep ascent of heaven*
> *Through peril, toil and pain.*

It will not turn the world upside down. In calm self-control it will sit and rot.

Yours,

SIMEON STYLITES.

Two Can Keep from Growing Old

Sir: The most beautiful thing ever said about marriage was said by that notable philosopher Humpty Dumpty, in *Alice Through the Looking Glass.* Humpty Dumpty is reproaching Alice for her rate of growth.

> "I never ask advice about growing," Alice said indignantly.
>
> "Too proud?" Humpty Dumpty inquired.
>
> Alice felt even more indignant at this suggestion. "I mean," she said, "that one cannot help growing old."
>
> "One can't, perhaps," said Humpty Dumpty, "but two can."

There you have it! One cannot help growing old, but *two* can. That is an Ode to Marriage in two words. It is not only beautiful, but true. We have all, praise be, seen youngsters who have kept each other from growing old through fifty years of marriage.

But now, lest you be drowned in a flood of sentimental tears at that lovely thought, I will proceed into detail and give you a few facts on some marvelous ways by which a loving wife can and does keep her husband from passing into the dissolution of senile repose.

Biologists tell us that one sign of life is irritability. If there is no irritability, there is no life. It is rather hard to irritate a stone. The higher we go in the scale of life, the greater the response to irritation. You never heard of a clam with a nervous breakdown. There is nothing to break down.

One life-preserving irritation which keeps intact the fighting spirit of youth in a husband is the well beloved voice in the car, making music like this: "See that red light ahead?" "This is a stop street." "You are too near the curb." Such music has no power to soothe the savage breast; it just makes it savager. And wards off old age.

One of our neighbors who will outlive Methuselah if irritation can bring it about is a man whose wife asks him every few days, "Did you see that article in the paper today about the correlation of lung cancer and cigarettes?" One day in a fine fettle of irritation he asked, "You like that word 'correlation.' Have you ever studied the correlation of conversation like yours and Reno, Nevada?"

The best recipe for a long life seems to be the mixture of affection and exasperation which every husband knows. Frances Warner writes truly that it is possible for a wife to irritate a man more by asking him three times whether he locked the back door than it is possible for his enemies to do with a libel.

Another thing that keeps a husband from going into a coma is to have his wife interrupt and edit his conversational showpieces.

Here's to a long life!

Yours,

SIMEON STYLITES.

PS. If any wife wants to make a rebuttal to these insults, come ahead.

Trivial

Sir: Here is a chance remark that looks as though Mrs. Malaprop might have made it. But it turns out to be quite a bit of sharp observation. In the novel *With Kitchen Privileges,* by Louise Andrews Kent, a cousin of the robust Mrs. Appleyard says to her, "I wish you wouldn't always look on the bright side of things, Susan, it's so trivial of you."

She did not make any mistake. "Trivial" is the right word for it. A persistent habit of always looking on the "bright side" of things is a thoroughly trivial occupation. Instead of a square look at things as they are, it is a kind of nursery play with fanciful creations. Of course, there is no great virtue in always looking at the dark side of things. Green glasses can give as distorted a view of the world as rose-colored ones. But for the long march Cassandra is a better (and safer) companion than Pollyanna. Cassandra's gloomy forebodings can become tiresome, but she never gets to be the completely paralyzing bore that Pollyanna does.

A preoccupation with the so-called "bright side" of things not only gives a warped view of affairs; it also cuts the nerve of any effort to better conditions. It is the Gloomy Gus who sees the dark side of things who is more likely to bestir himself to get something better.

When the eruption of Vesuvius got going in great form in A.D. 79, Pliny the Elder, a valiant looker-at-the-bright-side, kept announcing in reassuring tones, "Don't worry. Everything will be all right." Stout fellow! But it wasn't all right. Thomas Hardy had the true idea:

If a way to the better there be
It involves a clear look at the worst.

Which brings us to the subject of vaseline. Don't go! I really mean it! Some years ago there was a kind of photography which had quite a vogue among the aesthetic. Believe it or not, vaseline was put on a special kind of lens which was ground to produce a softening effect. The outlines of the thing photographed became blurred in a mist and the entire scene was somewhat out of focus. The whole effect was one of predawn unreality. It was lovely, but it obscured rather than illuminated. That is the kind of view of anything which the "always on the sunny side" folk get and report. The dreariest company in the world is a gathering of "bright side" lookers, desperately determined to be cheerful if it kills them. It doesn't kill them. It kills you.

Some of the most vicious enemies of Christianity today — far more deadly than all the Politburos put together — are the bumbling folk who have confused the Christian gospel with a trivial "looking at the bright side" of things. Christianity did not come into the world with a fixed, silly grin on its face and a vapid Cheerio on its lips. At its center was a cross. That heritage must be saved from being perverted by the Bright-side Boys, whether in the pulpit or out of it.

Yours,

SIMEON STYLITES.

The Constant Thermometer

Sir: When Eleanora Duse toured the United States to give dramatic performances, she was very fussy about her contract with her manager. She had heard of the horrors of the American climate, compared with that of her own sunny Italy. So she insisted that the manager agree to keep her room at the hotel or anywhere else at exactly 72 degrees all the time. That, in the days before the thermostats, presented the hotel people with quite a nice problem. But one ingenious workman solved it. "I fix," he said, and did. He substituted red ink for the mercury, putting it to show 72 degrees, and hung the doctored instrument on the wall of her room. The fixed thermometer was faithful and the great *artista* was happy. "America ees a great country," she said enthusiastically. "It rain, it snow, it friz, it boil, but the thermometer, he ees always 72." Only once did the spirit of skepticism raise its head, and then not very high. "Ees funny," she said, "how much colder 72 ees in Chicago than in New York."

The constant thermometer was a fine thing for Eleanora Duse's peace of mind, if not for heat of body. But with its unvarying 72 degrees it is a fair symbol of what is often the matter with us.

We today are used to constant thermometers. In fact we feel aggrieved if the thermometer varies one degree. We set the thermostat at a convenient figure on October 1, and keep it there until April 20. It is all too easy to transfer the constancy of temperature from the thermometer to the mind and spirit, and have them stay at unvarying equanimity, unchanging no matter what happens outside.

Of course we do not want a person's temper to go shooting up to 105 degrees every time the mail is late or he stubs his toe. But even that would make for more enlivening variety than a human constant thermometer, always showing 72 degrees.

Too many people have too large a dose of "peace,

perfect peace, in this dark world of sin" — peace in the perverse sense of the word. Not even what they read disturbs their equanimity, for they barricade their minds behind a wall of "wholesome" literature, which induces a very unwholesome state of soul. They sit with all the calm of Whistler's Mother, though decked out in quite different costumes.

The chief thing that is the matter with local politics is a too constant thermometer, never shooting up even in the face of corruption that smells to the sky or disregard of what liquor laws remain. There is a vicious sense to the text, "Great peace have those who love thy law and nothing shall offend them." There are citizens whom nothing offends. They always register a comfortable 72.

The same deathlike constancy is quite often found in the church.

There's Asia on the avenue,
And Europe on the street,
And Africa goes plodding by
Beneath my window seat.

But it never disturbs the spiritual anesthesia of some church people.

If anyone says, What do you want — *fever?* I answer, Good, you have grasped the point, even when it is mauled about by

Yours,

SIMEON STYLITES.

William Shakespeare's Ghost

Sir: In your wide reading of the world's great poetry, did you ever come across this immortal gem:

> *I dreamed that William Shakespeare's ghost*
> *Sat for a civil service post.*
> *The English paper for that year*
> *Was on the subject of "King Lear."*
> *William answered rather badly —*
> *You see he hadn't read his Bradley.*

It makes, I think, a very engaging picture to hang on the walls of imagination. There is poor William squirming at his desk, biting his pen, and scratching his head, baffled by the demand that he explain *King Lear* — all because he hadn't read Bradley's indispensable *Commentaries on Shakespeare.* How could a poor amateur like William be expected to know anything about Lear? What could he make of the towering superstructure erected on the foundation of his plays? What could he make of Hamlet, for instance, to whom some of the learned now ascribe such psychic ailments as Oedipus complex, ambivalence, overcompensation, inferiority complex, and agitated depression? He would certainly flunk *Hamlet.*

All this floated up to the surface of my mind from some depth where it had been lurking when I was recently struggling with a book of "dialectical theology"

— at least that is what a scholarly friend of mine told me it was. Not being an initiate in such matters, I wouldn't know. But I couldn't keep back the thought, "I wonder what Jesus would make of all this." I am sure that question is a little irreverent, but I couldn't keep it back. How would the Jesus we meet in the Gospels fare in an examination of some books of theology? I fear he would be lucky to get a C-plus.

Perhaps — to continue the irreverence — he would feel as Mr. Arthur Balfour said he did: "I am more or less happy when being praised, not very uncomfortable when being abused, but I have moments of uneasiness when being explained." Such "moments of uneasiness" come to any great leader or creator. Browning was dumfounded by many of the findings of the Browning societies. A few years ago a theologian wrote a book to show to that John Wesley was really a Calvinist. I would like to have seen John reading that one!

Of course, this kind of elucidation doesn't make much difference so far as Shakespeare or Browning is concerned. But it does make me wonder whether writing in the field of the Christian religion could not stay a little bit closer to what Jesus might understand. A musical friend of mine was talking not long ago about those pieces called "Variations on a Theme by Haydn" or "Bach" or "Schumann," and said that the variations are so many and so varied that the hearer wonders what the original theme was. Jesus has suffered so many variations at the hands of theologians that it is sometimes hard to imagine what the original words were.

Yours,

SIMEON STYLITES.

Drunk and Disorderly

Sir: I have several policemen friends. My motto is that of the Boy Scouts, "Be Prepared." So I try to be prepared for any emergency by having a few friends on the force. But I was not quite prepared for a jolt that one of my policemen friends gave me not long ago, not with a night-stick, but with a question.

He stopped me in the midst of street traffic and asked, "What is the degree which many preachers have which makes them Doctors?" I said, "It is usually a D.D." His face lit up. "That's funny," he said. "That is the commonest entry on every police blotter in the country, 'D.D.' Drunk and disorderly, it means."

I got safely out of traffic before reeling from that blow. Then, after partial recovery, my thoughts went back to the Book of Acts. It is remarkable that those were the first two charges brought continuously against the first preachers of the gospel. They were charged with being drunk. At the very first preaching of the gospel the charge was entered, "They were filled with new wine." And they were called "disorderly." We read the charge entered against them, "They dragged some of the brethren before the city authorities crying, 'These men who have turned the world upside down have come hither also.' "

Both charges were true. The drunk charge was true, of course, figuratively, as in the remark of the serving maid in Stephen Benét's beautiful Christmas play, *A Child Is Born,* she says of the shepherds, "They were drunk with the good news."

It would be a fine thing if we could gather all the preachers in the country into a sort of commencement exercise and say in solemn tones: "By virtue of the authority committed to me, I confer on you the degree of D. D. — Drunk and Disorderly." That is a very honorary degree. For if a preacher has never been called either drunk or disorderly, he may well go into a session of sweet silent thought with himself, and wonder if he is really in the apostolic succession.

Yours,

SIMEON STYLITES.

Viva la Negative!

Sir: Oft in the stilly night — well, more or less stilly — I have wondered, as has everyone else, at the mystery of language, in that there are so many words of which the negative is in common use, but which have no positives to go with them in contrast and opposition. You can make up your own list. A dictionary can be a lot of fun.

Here are a few. Being an editor, you are "distraught"

eight or ten times a day. But are you ever "traught"? I doubt it. We know a lot of "innocuous" things. Did you ever hear of a "nocuous" one? We say that a person is "ungainly." But do we ever see a "gainly" one? "He is 'uncouth,' " we say of a man. Why not call the opposite number a "couth" person? But there is no positive of the word. We speak of a day of "infamy." Why not a day of "famy," to remember with pride? Thinking all this over, I get "disgruntled." I would like to be "gruntled" for a change.

Perhaps this kink in language is part of something larger — the lure of the negative. It seems easier to handle. So many people are heavy on the negative, while the positive is not only weak but often nonexistent. Someone has observed that the vocabulary of invective is so much more extensive than the vocabulary of praise. If you want to call a man a scoundrel, a score of vivid words rush to your lips. But if you want to call him "a good man," you say that and you are all through, unless there is a Roget close at hand.

This allure of the negative is right at the center of a lot of things. Think of the highly articulate groups who spend eighteen hours a day denouncing communism. We are all against communism. But for some people anticommunism has become a holy religion, the ten commandments of which are all loud negatives. One might expect, naïvely perhaps, that such opposition to communism would generate a positive devotion to democracy. Does it? Don't make me laugh! These antis have no positives in their vocabulary of hatred — mere hatred never generates great positives.

Too many Christians have bogged down in negatives and have few or no great affirmatives. They are "agin" something, but are really *for* little or nothing. Hugh Black used to tell of a little boy in Scotland who, on his first day at school, was asked what was the religion of his family. He replied, "Please sir, we don't drink beer." Even those who would roundly applaud non-beer-drinking as a sound idea must admit that it lacks something as a religion. But that answer describes much negative Christianity. One fine result of the growing observance of Reformation Day by Protestant churches is the emphasis that has been laid on the first syllable of the word "Protestant." *Pro* means *for*. In a time marked by a "hunger for affirmatives," negatives, no matter how vociferous, are a vain thing.

Innocuously yours,

SIMEON STYLITES.

Riffraff

Sir: The pastor of St. John's-by-the-Gas-Station was in the drugstore having a third cup of coffee and looking as pleased with himself as a cat that has just swallowed a canary.

"What has happened to you?" I asked as I sat down beside him.

"I had a good scrap yesterday, and there is nothing

like a slug fest to keep up one's interest in the ministry," he told me.

"Whom — if that is the right grammar — did you slug?" I inquired.

"Some of my church officials. I was just trying to avoid the woe that is promised to fall on you when all men speak well of you. And, boy, did I succeed! You should have heard them! St. John's is on the way to becoming a Christian church. We are running out of Bank Presidents and Chairmen of Boards as new members and have had to take in *people*. Some of our officials don't like the idea. They said to me, 'If you go on taking in more riffraff and rag, tag, and bobtail, St. John's will be losing its character.'

" 'It might save its soul,' I put in. That didn't help any.

"Yesterday I let 'em have it. I told them the old parable about Jesus and the social undesirables — the one, you know, by Frank Harris, of all people. I said, 'This is for you. I hope you get the point.' You remember it? It goes like this:

" 'Every morning St. Peter found in heaven a horde of undesirable aliens, whom he was certain he had never admitted at the regular hours. Some had never been baptized, some were ignorant of the Bible, many were soiled and damaged souls who clearly had no right in the celestial precincts. He decided to discover just how this leakage had occurred. So in the darkness he prowled about the ramparts of heaven. At last he discovered a dark corner where a few stones had been removed from the wall since his last inspection an hour before. A crowd was stealthily creeping in. He rushed at them with indignation, but was amazed to find the Savior there, helping some of the cripples over the wall. "I'm sorry, Peter," the Lord said. "I know it's against the rules. These poor souls are not all they should be. Some were never baptized. Some of them are not quite orthodox in their opinions of me, and all of them are miserable sinners. But they are my special friends and I want them here.' "

"So I think they got the point. Do you know any 'riffraff' that I might go out after?"

That's what he said.

Yours,

SIMEON STYLITES.

What Happened to the Kitchen?

Sir: She was showing a visitor the wonders of her new Pullman kitchen. At the climax her face registered ecstasy. "See," she cried, "it is so compact! I can stand in the center and reach everything." And she did. The visitor was a deplorable cynic, immune to enthusiasm. "It is well named," he growled. "Pullman. It had just as much room as a Pullman lower berth. You can reach everything there, too."

Which raises the order of the day: What happened to the kitchen? It was once the center of the home, the seat of family life when there was a lot of it and the term was not merely a nostalgic expression. Of course, we all know the score of answers to the question What happened to the kitchen? History happened to it, and a lot of sociology and industrial progress. It was diminished and outmoded by improvements for living, with the result that the improvements supplanted the living they were supposed to serve. The wood or coal range succumbed to the electric stove, and all the other compact gadgets ended the transformation of the kitchen into the "kitchenette." (Watch out for words ending in "ette." They are usually phony.)

The kitchen was where people lived. It had inconveniences, measured by the standards of a time when convenience is the chief end of existence. But it had life. Other things besides opening tin cans and snapping electric switches went on there. The earlier homes showed the right idea. The center was where things happened, in the kitchen. The front parlor was a mausoleum where state affairs were held — funerals and formal calls and other painful occasions. There was cooking in the kitchen. Well, I mustn't get into that. But I warn you I am doing research for a monograph on the greatest failure of American industry — failure to make a real loaf of bread on an investment of billions of dollars. Today, in biblical language, if our son asks for bread do we give him a stone? No, we do worse. We give him something laughingly called bread, a mass of air surrounded by soggy dough.

Then at night there was the table with the oil lamp. This was true not only in the country but right in crowded New York, too. In his book of recollections of his youth, *A Walker in the City,* Alfred Kazin salutes the kitchen thus:

> As a child, I felt we lived in the kitchen, to which the other four rooms were annexed. The kitchen held our lives together. My mother worked in it all day long; we ate in it all meals except the Passover *seder.* I did my home work and first writing at the kitchen table.

There is no use just weeping by the wailing wall. We might try to move the kitchen into the living room. That is, transfer the real social and spiritual values of the kitchen of an earlier day into what ought to be, and often is not, the living room. The trouble with the living room is that it is, all too often, more like a bus station, a place of departure for members of the family. More things of a cohesive nature must happen in the living room. We need social inventions for the living room to match the mechanical inventions of the kitchen.

Nostalgic nonsense? All right. But I still think that if there were more kids in the kitchen, there might be fewer in the reform school.

Yours,

SIMEON STYLITES.

An Orchid for the Weather Man

Sir: The Man of the House, before leaving for the office, was listening to the broadcast of the weather man. He listened patiently to what seemed to be an encyclopedia article on meteorology. As paragraph followed paragraph, his frown became deeper and his face fiercer. Finally the explosion burst: "Well, of all the blank blank idiots! What does he think he is doing, writing a book on cosmic rays? And what does he think we are, blank blank graduate students? Here I want to know whether it is going to rain today. Does he tell me? Don't make me laugh! He gives a lecture on cold pressure systems 2000 miles away in Montana, or a warm air mass down in Louisiana shaping up to meet in a world series battle with an iceberg coming down from Hudson's Bay. Good night!"

He had a grievance, even if it did not call for so many blanks. All of us, eager to find out whether it will rain on the Fourth of July picnic, are frustrated to be told that the precipitation around Beatrice, Nebraska, was point 6, or that the isobars running down from Denver to Santa Fe reveal high pressure and that small-craft warnings are posted at Galveston, Texas. When all we want to know is whether it is going to rain in Pittsburgh! Consequently the weather man is reviled; he covers too much territory when we are in a hurry.

I rise to the defense of this public servant. I present

him with an accolade, or at least an orchid. I even propose that he be ordained a minister of the gospel, or at least a licensed exhorter. For every morning, in his reports of high pressure or cold air masses half a continent away, he preaches the gospel of national interdependence, and that is a gospel much needed. His eye, swinging from Wyoming to Maine, enforces the truth that no man, no city, no state lives to him- or itself. We are members one of another when it comes to weather. There is no special weather for Parkersburg, West Virginia, that is not affected by what is happening with the weather in South Dakota or Alabama. The country, to a large extent, is tied together in one bundle of life, for better or worse. The lecture on meteorology becomes a symbol of a larger truth that whatever affects one group in the nation has its effect on others. If there is a low pressure area in buying power, it will have its disastrous effect in other areas. If full citizenship is denied to one group, all citizenship is insecure. We rise and fall together.

The same is true of a wider weather map, the world. What happens in the World is as near as our front door, and it soon comes in at every front door in the land. There is no East that is far. The Far East and the Near East are as near to every home as is every 18-year-old boy in that home.

Christopher Morley summed it up: "The man about town must become the man about planet."

Yours,

SIMEON STYLITES.

Travel by the Train

Sir: Dean Inge, of St. Paul's Cathedral, is not remembered primarily as a poet. But he was once moved to compose four lines in adaptation of a hymn which are cherished by addicts of surprise endings. He said that the favorite hymn of many church people was:

They climbed the steep ascent of heaven
Through peril, toil and pain:
O God, to us may grace be given
To travel by the train.

As one surveys the ecclesiastical scene in some places, one must admit that train travel has been heavy. The painful ascent to heaven through peril and toil has given way to more comfortable travel on a Vista Dome Express, which permits an interesting view of the scenery, along with rest to the muscles of the soul. These passengers do not ask to be

. . . carried to the skies
On flowery beds of ease.

All they ask is to ride in a Pullman.

A century ago Nathaniel Hawthorne noted a change in travel habits in his story "The Celestial Railroad," which tells how later Pilgrims rolled comfortably along the old road of Pilgrim's Progress, with no stops in the Valley of Humiliation or Doubting Castle and no battle with the fiend, Apollyon, or with Giant Despair. There was, however — wasn't there? — a stopover at Vanity Fair.

Elimination of peril and toil has made great strides since Bunyan's and even Hawthorne's day. Old words, such as "*agonize* to enter the strait gate," have been discarded as obsolete. In a world devoted to comfort it is fitting to have a comfortable religion. As one woman said ecstatically to another, "We have the most up-to-date church in the country. We have inner springs in the pew cushions." Evidently more attention to inner springs than to the inner man. Perhaps fifty-two sermons a year on "You, too, can be a Big Booming Success."

A comfortable, enjoyable religion is sketched in a poem by William Blake in his *Songs of Experience:*

But if at Church they would give us some Ale,
And a pleasant fire our souls to regale,
We'd sing and we'd pray all the live-long day,
Nor ever once wish from the Church to stray.

Then the Parson might preach, and drink, and sing,
And we'd be as happy as birds in the spring; . . .

And God, like a father rejoicing to see
His children as pleasant and happy as he,
Would have no more quarrel with the Devil or the Barrel,
But kiss him, and give him both drink and apparel.

That is extreme, and more than a bit vulgar. Blake seems to have written it as a protest against a religion of gloom. But it is not too distant a caricature of what would seem to many an ideal religion, with perils and penalties neatly eliminated. Great progress has been made for many since the days when "some were tortured . . . Others suffered mocking and scourging, and even chains and imprisonment. They were stoned, they were sawn in two . . . destitute, afflicted, ill-treated." Instead of those doleful words, it can now be written: "Through faith they dismissed all their worries, achieved a harmonious adjustment to the world, and obtained a state of beatific relaxation."

Train time! All aboard!

Yours,

SIMEON STYLITES.

Pigheaded

Sir: In every church body — synod, annual conference, or state association — there is a Historical Society. These societies meet annually and adjourn for lack of a quorum. Occasionally they preserve one of John Wesley's shoe buckles or one of Alexander Campbell's riding boots, but such are rare finds.

My heart has been touched by thinking of these unemployed historians, so I am giving them something important to do: Start immediately making a collection of the human interest and humorous stories in the tradition of the church, stories that will otherwise soon drop down between the cracks and be lost forever. The real life and spirit of a church are found not only, or, often, not so much, in solemn platforms and pronouncements as in seemingly unimportant happenings and sayings.

Mr. Chesterton somewhere observed that what holds families together is not so much the Ten Commandments or undying love as family jokes; these are esoteric bonds, like secret passwords, known only to the family and showing life as it was lived. That is almost true.

How many stories were lost when Bishop McConnell died! Who can ever forget the flash in his eye when he told of an irate Methodist who, right after the "Inter-Church Report on the Steel Strike" was published, wrote Bishop McConnell in immortal words, "You are a first-class skunk!" and then signed the letter, "Your brother in Christ"? That tells us a lot about the steel strike! How much we owe to those who preserved Luther's table talk! And how we would like to know whether St. Paul ever got the cloak and books he sent for! Not as important as the eighth chapter of Romans, but a nice bit of history just the same.

A few things like these ought not to perish. One is that bit of tradition of Drew Theological Seminary. The beloved Dr. Samuel F. Upham lay dying; friends and relatives were gathered about the bed. The question arose whether he was still living or not. Someone advised, "Feel his feet. No one ever died with warm feet." Dr. Upham opened an eye and said, "John Hus did." Those were his last words, and glorious ones too. They tell a lot about the relation of humor to faith.

I hate to think of a story about the late Bishop E. L. Waldorf of the Methodist Church dropping out of sight. When the Bishop opened a Republican national convention in Chicago he made an exceedingly long prayer. As he went on and on, Heywood Broun, who was in the press pit, right in front of the platform, watched with growing amazement and finally exclaimed, "My Gawd! It's a filibuster!" That tells more about customs in prayer than you will get in any official history.

My last bit of evidence is admittedly trivial, so I like it. It is true too, like everything else I write. Dr. Christian F. Reisner was speaking at the opening of a retreat for ministers at West Point several years ago. He was thrilled by the fine attendance and spoke of the value of retreats, recalling the words of Jesus, "Come ye apart and rest awhile." Then, after a dramatic pause, he said, "It is a great thing to see three hundred men come apart."

Yours,

SIMEON STYLITES.

PS. Note to all publishers: This would be a gold mine!

Effective Speaking for Wives

Sir: As though we did not have enough troubles already, what with the hydrogen bomb, and the open season for pushing the lawn mower and grubbing in the garden upon us, now comes a nasty threat from Canada. Hitherto, Canada has been a peaceful neighbor, but the present threat may change all that, and end the love-and-good-wishes era. Item, to wit, the Canadian Press relays the grim news that in Calgary, Alberta, a course in "Effective Speaking" has been offered housewives by the parks department in cooperation with the Junior Chamber of Commerce, and the wives have flocked into it. That's the trouble with these Juniors, they don't know it is loaded!

"Effective Speaking for Wives," my eye! What wife ever needed a course in effective speaking? She needs it as badly as a robin needs a course in singing, or a cricket needs a course in chirping! Don't they know in Calgary how this thing may spread over the United States?

Every husband agrees with old Thomas Fuller that "silence is a fine jewel for a woman." He would like to see his wife decked out in such shining jewels in necklace, bracelets, and rings. William E. Gladstone was said to have been miraculous in his presentation of the national budget to Parliament. Any husband would match his wife anytime against Gladstone in presenting the month's family budget.

Of course, the wife's voice is the sweetest noise in nature, but why try to gild the lily by giving lessons? A wife has mastered all the varieties of effective speech listed in classic phrase by Shakespeare in *As You Like It*. Here is the repertoire. The order of the day is that highly controversial subject, "This is a good night for cutting the grass, isn't it?" The lord and master, in a manner of speaking, replies, "No. I've had a hard day at the office, and I am all worn out." Then, all the different styles of speech, listed by Shakespeare:

The Retort Courteous: "You poor thing, I hope you live till the doctor can get here."

The Quip Modest: "I'm sure of it. You had better watch your step, for you are just fading away to a mere two hundred pounds."

The Reproof Valiant: "What do you suppose *I* have been doing all day, sleeping? While you were sitting in an air-conditioned office!"

The Countercheck Quarrelsome: "If I got 'all poohed out' as easily as you do, this house would be a shambles."

The Lie Circumstantial: "I know all about your hard day at the office. Two hours for lunch and a ball game!"

The Lie Direct: "All worn out! You're as husky as a truck horse!"

This is just an overture to the real orations of the evening.

I am not in favor of breaking off diplomatic relations with Canada. But I do urge the officials not to let this poisonous idea of courses in effective speaking for wives get over the border.

How about wives giving lessons in effective speech to mute, inglorious Miltons of husbands?

Yours,

SIMEON STYLITES.

A Plea for Disorderly Conduct

Sir: My desk has been straightened up again. The noble Christian woman who performs that biweekly atrocity known as "setting things to rights" does not realize what neatly arranged chaos she imposes on what had been logical and intelligible disorder. As a result I am lost. So is everything else. I can't find the gas bill. That is all right with me. But there are more dire consequences. I can't find the coupon I got from a train conductor, redeemable for ten cents at any ticket office. So you see it is a serious matter, a tragic theme for Sophocles.

Of all the heresies which have plagued the faithful, that ancient proverb that "order is heaven's first law" is the one most deserving of anathemas. It was invented by prim systematizers for the irritation of the godly. If "order" is heaven's first law, I do not want to go to heaven. Do not interrupt me. I said it first — I will be spared that necessity.

As an expert in Freudian lore, you will recognize this wail as a rationalization by a disorderly mind.

Just the same, I think that an argument could be framed for the defense of a fruitful disorder. Go back to a desk for a moment. God bless the man who first said, "The more litter, the more literature." True. Give a man six square feet of cleared and spotless mahogany desk before him, with twelve sharpened pencils and three pens in their proper places, and he will never write anything more profound than "Mary had a little lamb."

History is on my side. A passion for order, for neat arrangement, though the heavens fall, has often prevented heaven on earth. Isn't it true that the great inquisitors have always come from the ranks of the great systematizers? The morning stars of the Reformation were put out by a zeal for ecclesiastical order. After all, the Hitler government was, on the surface (where conventional order operates) a very orderly affair. The Allied armies found the Nazis' papers filed perfectly, all ready for Mr. Churchill to use in writing his memoirs. Everything neatly arranged — Jews in concentration camps, Elite troops in comfortable barracks. Spotless order has been used time out of mind to cover up all kinds of injustice.

As I read the Good Book it seems to me to have evidence that God is on the side of the spontaneous, the impulsive, the unrehearsed, the thing that cannot be fitted into man's pattern. We read that His thoughts are not our thoughts, and much in the record shows that they are not. The preaching of the cross was foolishness to the Greeks. The crucifixion was a very disorderly thing to the neat and reasonable Greek mind. Consider the miserable axiom, endlessly repeated in parrot fashion to the despair of children, "A place for everything and everything in its place." Nonsense! There was a place in the organized life of Judea for babies to be born. That place was not in a stable. But there it was, a Baby in a stable. Highly irregular!

In the whole matter of industrial conflict, of strikes, if order is our first passion, we can push all human values down out of sight. The most orderly place on earth is a cemetery.

Perhaps more divine disorder might save our church services from dying of too much regularity and bring more free and spontaneous movement of the spirit into them. I dread the announcement on bulletin boards, "Service Sunday morning at 11 o'clock, as usual." Isn't that what is the matter with us—too much "as usual"?

My spiritual guide (and a tough assignment he has) recently preached at a Lenten service at a strange church. When he arrived the choir leader told him apologetically: "I had to change the processional hymn you sent me. It was in three-four time, poor marching rhythm. If the choir followed that music, they would have had to go dancing down the aisle." The preacher thought a moment and said, "Might be a good idea." It might, at that.

Yours,

SIMEON STYLITES.

A Growl from the Pew

Sir: "I've been growled at," said the pastor of St. John's-by-the-Gas-Station, the words coming out from behind a corrugated frown.

I looked him over for tooth marks and did not see any. "Well," I said, "at least you haven't been bitten."

"No," he admitted, "but it was almost a bite, and besides I don't like growls. He wasn't growling at me alone, but at the clergy in general, including me. I met an old friend on the bus and he fastened on to me like a wolf after a scared rabbit.

" 'I went to church yesterday,' the man said, 'and have been groping in the fog ever since. It was a good service; the hymns were good; the Lord's Prayer was good — I have always approved of it. But the sermon was a series of skillful maneuvers in a vacuum. It reminded me of the can of coffee on the shelf at home, on which it says "vacuum packed." That was it, all right. The points were packed in a vacuum. Clouds of general statements up in the stratosphere and not a single raindrop came down to water the earth. What's the matter with you fellows?

" 'While it was going on, I got to thinking,' he said, 'of the hot water heater we had put into our cottage up at the lake this summer. When I got there in August it was all installed, a shining thing, white, covered with something called Permaglass. It was a beauty, but it wasn't running. I wanted to use it, and then to my joy I saw attached to it what I thought was a set of directions. That is where I made my mistake. It wasn't a set of directions, but a set of tributes, beautifully printed in red and blue, telling me that the heater was (1) safe, (2) quick, (3) efficient, (4) tamper-proof, (5) economical, (6) dependable. I said yes, yes, but how does the thing work? What do I do to use it to get some hot water? Not a word on what to do. I would have traded all six eloquent tributes for three clear words of direction.

" 'It was the same way with the sermon. Tributes galore — tributes to the Bible, to the prophets all the way from Amos to Kagawa; endorsements of the Christian faith, as though it were a new miracle drug. Heavens, I will grant all that before the tributes begin! What I would like to know is how religion works. How do I turn it on? What can I do with it?'

"I interrupted the growl long enough to tell him that the king of the wise men, Gaius Glenn Atkins, once said that the minister's forgotten word is 'how.'

"That was a bull's-eye, he admitted, and then kept barking right on. 'Suppose,' he said, 'that instead of a road sign that pointed clearly, Milwaukee to the left and Madison to the right, there was set up a beautiful framed picture of one of Turner's sunsets, or the "Angelus," or, worse still, one of Picasso's nightmares. How could you get anywhere? Can't you give us fewer sunsets and more road directions?'

"I said in rebuttal, 'This is my stop.' It wasn't, but I got off anyway."

And so will I.

Yours,

SIMEON STYLITES.

The Cult of the Hairy Ape

Sir: America, the sociologists tell us, is a land of cults. I guess they are right. Ellen Glasgow in her volume of memoirs, *The Woman Within,* has given the name "Cult of the Hairy Ape" to one of the most active and vicious of our star-spangled cults. By that phrase she denotes the "assault on the intellect" which marked the 1930's in America. In those years it was usually labeled the "mucker pose." It marks and blights our time too. The "Cult of the Hairy Ape" has many devotees at its altars. It boasts a disdain and contempt for intelligence and a glorification of the lowbrow—a very pleasant technique, for its vogue enables a person, instead of apologizing for his ignorance and vulgarity, to exult in them and often to compel people who know better to bow down to them.

We can hear the worship ritual of this cult in the denunciation of the "egghead." Anyone possessed of a mature intelligence is an "egghead," and by so much an object of scorn. It is dangerous for a statesman, if he is running for office, to be known as a man who can rub two thoughts together and produce a luminous idea. With a large number of voters he will do much better if he insists that he is one of the near-illiterate and hits the cultural level of a Bathhouse John or a Hinky Dink.

A perfect illustration of a high priest of this cult is the humorist H. Allen Smith. He says he glories in his ignorance (he has much to glory in). He boasts of his "peasant tastes"; he prefers Crosby to Flagstad and in poetry proclaims himself a "Shooting-of-Dan-McGrew" man.

The whole cult is the barbarian invasion so well described a generation ago by the Spaniard Ortega y Gasset, who warned that Western civilization was threatened by barbarians within. The barbarian is the "mass man," a term that is so terrifyingly familiar today — the man who has no high standards of any sort for himself and takes pleasure in his mediocrity.

This throws into vivid light the most important source of juvenile delinquency: our values are catching up with us. So many prefer a pose of toughness to any trace of tenderness, which is a "sissy" trait; so many prefer violence to reasonableness, and disdain anything resembling culture. We need not be surprised if the oncoming generation has noticed our values and adopted them.

One bit of counterrevolution might start at the table in the living room — if there is a table, except the ones on which the TV and the radio stand. Try this on your imagination, from Agnes Repplier:

A blessed custom of my infancy ordained that every living room should be dominated by a good-sized center table, and that on this center table should repose those ponderous illustrated volumes for which our parents spent vast sums of money, and which we children never tired of examining.

Might be worth trying.

Yours,

SIMEON STYLITES.

Tiddlywinks

Sir: Everyone is entitled, just to keep his mind in balance (if possible), to slip away once in a while from this hydrogen world. It is good medicine to get back, in imagination at least, to a time when the world was stable and hydrogen was only a beneficent part of H_2O. One of the most stable of all the eras in which to roam is the Victorian era, when everything seemed as unshakable as the Rock of Ages — at least until Darwin began to erupt.

A good book to make the trip on is *A Pleased Girl,* by Lady Emily Luytens, published in 1954. It is the true story of a very young girl in the mid-century, told mostly in letters which she wrote to a charming clergyman fifty-eight years her senior. It contains an exclamation worth recalling. She is describing to her elderly correspondent the thrill of the year, the amazing discovery of — tiddlywinks. She wrote, "I have just discovered the most wonderful game in all the world — tiddlywinks!"

That childish wonder and ecstasy bring into view a long procession of crazes, hobbies, ideas, which have streaked across the sky of a period like so many meteorites, to be greeted with exuberant acclaim as the most marvelous thing that ever was, with just as thrilled an amazement as the young girl felt over that wonder of the world, tiddlywinks. Most of them are forgotten now. But if we recall some of these flaming ephemeral wonders it may help us to see with the right proportion some of the wonders of our own day. Like the world-shaking game of tiddlywinks, they too will have their day and cease to be, or at least be reduced to size.

This is certainly true in the religious field. There is no realm of thought and interest in which there have been more sets of ideas, greeted successively as the most wonderful thing in the world.

Can you remember back — not too far back — when, to quite a large number of church people, Buchmanism was the current tiddlywinks, destined to change the whole face of the church? The face is much the same today. Some backward minds were not convinced that "conversion" had been invented by the Oxford Group, and some stubborn souls even claimed to have come across references to it in an ancient tome, the book of Acts.

Farther back there was Group Discussion. That has left gains of enduring worth to the church. But at its advent it was hailed as the New Messiah by many. So great was its vogue that there was sharp point to the quip of Dean Willard L. Sperry, that if the vogue of Group Discussion had been as strong in Paul's day, when the Philippian jailer asked, "What must I do to be saved?" Paul would have had to answer, "Well, what do *you* think about it?"

Now there is "Existentialism." Not everybody talking about it knows what it means, but it is nice to know that it "exists." Much more democratic and widespread is the current tiddlywinks, the Cult of Comfort or Peace of Mind, the "Take-it-Easy, Boys," revelation. And don't forget "Group Dynamics." Those potent words always remind me of the Four Horsemen of the Notre Dame football team. They were a dynamic group all right.

All in all, this procession gives a picture of the progress of the church — something like Eliza crossing the river, leaping from cake of ice to cake of ice. The church seems to leap from one new craze or hobby to another.

For which we can thank God and take courage. This succession of leaps has kept the church from getting immobilized on dead center and from going static. It is good to greet each new interest or idea as "the greatest ever in the world" — so long as we do not confuse it with the imperishable gospel which is, we are told, the same yesterday, today, and forever.

Yours,

SIMEON STYLITES.

"I've Got a Little List"

Sir: The pastor of St. John's-by-the-Gas-Station was whistling merrily as he walked down the street. I recognized a familiar tune from *The Mikado,* "I've Got a Little List."

I said to him, "I recognize from your disturbance of the atmosphere that you have a little list."

"That I have," he replied gleefully. "I've got a little list of people in a church who are an irritant to every pastor. In fact, they are usually pests. I do not advocate calling in a pest exterminator, but they should be identified and at least included in the litany, 'Good Lord, deliver us!'

"One is the highly loquacious church member — I am not entirely sure that the female of this species is more deadly than the male — who is always recalling at length, and with warm emotion, how much better everything was when Dr. Demosthenes was pastor. 'Ah, those were the days! [Sigh.] He packed them in like sardines — a church full, 800 in the pews, scores standing at the back. [The official records show an average attendance of 375.] There were giants in those days!'

"Then there is Brother P. Nurious, that stout pillar who made his pledge to the church twenty-five years ago and has not made any change or shadow of turning upward since. He feels strongly that the command in the Old Testament not to remove the ancient landmark also applies to an ancient pledge to the church. So it still stands, an emblem of hope to a needy world — a dollar a Sunday.

"But do not forget the ladies. There is the elect lady who gripes because the pastor hasn't called on her for a month. She hasn't revised her thinking — if that is the right word — since the merry-go-round days when it was the accepted thing for a pastor to go round and round the parish calling on all the members, working his feet so fast that he had no time to work his head. When her pastor said, 'Why don't you do some parish calling yourself?' she was insulted.

"Then there is the trustee, the Watchdog of the Treasury, who will block any project for which the hard cold cash is not in hand — in clutching hands. There he stands, steadfast, immovable, always thwarting the work of the Lord. What if the money is pledged or can be raised? He has a crushing rejoinder to that: 'My mother always said never buy anything till you have the money in your hand.' So every day is Mother's Day to him. Most of the time of pastor and officials is spent devising ingenious detours around this steadfast servant of God.

"I have to get a bus," he said, "but don't forget

the Constitutional Lawyer. He is the modern equivalent of St. Paul's thorn in the flesh. He is a messenger of Satan to buffet the church. And he wields a wicked buffet. 'Yes,' he points out, 'it is a fine idea to think of taking in a refugee family. But watch your step! The by-laws do not authorize any such expenditure.' But when Brother Jones said, 'I don't see anything in the by-laws authorizing you, either,' he was peeved."

I said, expecting a violent disclaimer, "I suppose you have me on the list too?"

"Brother Abou Ben Adam," he said solemnly, "your name leads all the rest."

Yours,

SIMEON STYLITES.

King of Indoor Sports

Sir: Not to be mysterious about it, and in the hope of starting a nasty scrap, may I announce dogmatically that the King of Indoor Sports is not Poker, or Scrabble, or Watching TV, but Reading Aloud in the Family. And it has become a Lost Art, worse luck!

I can hear a mythical reader gasp, "Great grief, what a Back Number poor old Simeon is!" To which insult I make two replies. The first is: "Just step outside and say that again." The second is: "There's a lot to be said for back numbers. I have a friend who has a mess of back numbers of an old magazine in light-blue covers, the *Strand Illustrated* of London, containing installments of *The Adventures of Sherlock Holmes.* I would match that against anything that reaches the newsstands tomorrow, not even excepting *True Confessions.*"

Of course there are dangers of painful *ennui* in reading aloud — when it is done pompously or officiously. James Thurber in his *Decalogue for Wives* recognizes these dangers of family torture. He tells wives how to listen to a husband reading aloud, whether a blow-by-blow description of a prize fight or yesterday's stock market quotations. He warns against biting the finger nails, tapping the feet, or interrupting the reading to tell the Beloved that his socks do not match.

Nevertheless, reading aloud is a great indoor sport when any one of a hundred "right" books is chosen *and* the object is not improvement of the mind (how many crimes have been committed in that name!) but just fun. What else can so powerfully draw a family together in a strong bond of imagination?

And what else can match reading aloud for developing the imagination? It is a cardinal mistake for parents to stop reading to the kids when Susie and Willie learn to read in a poor, lisping, stammering tongue. Susie and Willie need training in what Shelley called "to imagine what we see."

From movies and TV we get facts, or alleged facts. These can be dead. The superiority of imagination over crass detail is well shown in Arthur Knight's reflections on the film version of *Oklahoma!,* lamenting its firm grasp of the obvious:

> This *Oklahoma!* [film] insists on the obvious. This screen can take in miles and miles of Oklahoma? All right. Let's show them miles and miles of Oklahoma . . . The song says the "corn is as high as an elephant's eye." All right. We'll just hold up production till the corn gets there (as a program note proudly exclaims). Imagination, fantasy, freedom . . . have been rigorously excluded.

Youth is defrauded when everything is all spelled out. Superman and Heigh-ho, Silver! make a poor show compared to the workout the imagination gets in reading the *Tale of Two Cities* or even Mayne Reid. (Anybody remember Mayne Reid?) More than that. There is real point for every parent in the cartoon of a father in a chair in the living room reading a book entitled *Why Johnny Can't Read* while Johnny is looking at TV.

A horrible vision of the future, unveiled a few days ago, makes it all the more important to revive the lost art of reading. We are told that already 35 per cent of TV offerings is made up of movies, and that in another year it will be 70 per cent. A bleak desert of soap and horse opera. The soap is more deadly than the horse.

Another recent cartoon showed a boy looking at a pair of book ends, with books between them, on top of a TV set. The boy asks: "Is that a new kind of antenna?" No, Willie, that is a very old kind of antenna, for the reception of ideas. A very dependable kind too.

Let's see, kids, when we left off yesterday Jean Valjean had just turned into a blind alley with the police after him. Let's go!

Yours,

SIMEON STYLITES.

Coldness of Mind

Sir: Are you ever troubled by your mind slipping into reverse? There is something the matter with my gear shift. Instead of moving right along in orderly fashion, from neutral into first and into second, my mind goes right from first into reverse. I get to thinking: How would this idea look in reverse or upside down? Should I see a psychiatrist?

For instance, some time ago when I heard that beautiful prayer from the *Book of Common Prayer* asking for "deliverance from wandering of mind and coldness of heart," I said to myself: "All right. That is what we need to be delivered *from*. What should we be delivered *to?"* Obviously, I thought, into the opposite. The right condition would be, "coldness of mind and wandering of heart." I still think I may have something. In an ideal life, the heart should wander and the mind remain cool.

Of course, the first thought of a cold mind does not allure us. To say that a person is a "cold fish" is no compliment. But just leave the fish out of it and stay on land. A "cold mind" is the most beautiful instrument on earth. It is a precision instrument, and how the world needs that kind of instrument! It can do clear, hard, accurate thinking, not deflected by emotionalism nor warmed by sentimentalism till it grows soft. The mind does not work surely when it has a 104 degree temperature.

A woman facing an operation told a friend, "I do hope I have a sympathetic surgeon." The friend replied: "You're crazy! I wouldn't care whether my surgeon had a warm heart or not. What I would care about would be whether he has his stuff down cold. When I am wheeled into the operating room, I do not want a surgeon with his eyes so blinded with sympathetic tears that he cannot see the right place to begin the opening exercises." Amen! A cold mind saves us from thinking with the emotions, always a terrible thing, or from that exercise Hitler loved so well, thinking with the blood. He demonstrated that when people think with their blood, it results in rivers of blood.

The prayer is right: wandering of mind is bad, and an enemy of true prayer and real thinking. When the mind wanders like a Mexican jumping bean, nothing happens but chaos. It is the *heart* that should wander, out into other lives and other places, making sympathetic journeys which can find places where the mind should work.

When the heart does not journey with dedicated imagination into other situations, a mean kind of slavery results. I have watched with interest the growing class of serfs in America. You see lots of them in our finest suburbs. That word is carefully chosen — a serf is a person attached to the ground; he cannot leave it. Our American serfs are attached to small pieces of ground, their front and back yards. Every Sunday is given to those small patches of ground, religiously and irreligiously. Their only service of worship is done with a lawn mower. To them, the yards are the whole big blooming world. Alexander the Something or Other freed the serfs in Russia. Someone ought to do it for the serfs in the United States. They are chained to a piece of ground.

Yours,

SIMEON STYLITES.

Pilate's Washbowl

Sir: Have you ever read Walter Rauschenbusch's account of what happened to Pilate's washbowl? Rauschenbusch's piece is never out of date; in fact it is every day more and more pertinent in its picture of the excuses which people and organizations give for doing nothing even to try to block any kind of wrong.

Rauschenbusch's is one of many speculations about what happened to several symbols which appear in the story of the trial and crucifixion of Jesus. Lloyd Douglas did it with *The Robe.* A hardly medieval parable on the thirty pieces of silver dramatizes the idea that whenever there was a dark betrayal of the commands of the Master, it was paid for by one of the original pieces of silver given to Judas, which came down through the centuries.

Here is Walter Rauschenbusch writing sixty years ago:

> On the eve of the day [of the crucifixion] the Washbowl disappeared from the palace. Nobody knows who took it. Some accused Judas Iscariot of selling it; but that is plainly a libel, because Judas was honest enough to go and hang himself. At any rate, ever since that time, the Washbowl is abroad in the land, carried by infernal hands wherever it is needed, and men are constantly joining the invisible choir which performs its imperceptible ablutions therein. The statesman who suppresses principles because they might endanger the success of his party; the good citizen who will have nothing to do with politics; the editor who sees a righteous cause misrepresented and says nothing, because it might injure the

circulation; the deacon who sees a clique undermining a pastor's position and dares not create a disturbance; the preacher who sees Dives exploiting Lazarus and dares not tell him to quit, because Dives contributes to his salary; the Sunday school superintendent who sees a devoted teacher punctured by pinpricks of well bred jealousy and dares not champion her; all these are using Pilate's Washbowl. Listen! do you hear the splash of water near to you? The Devil is pouring it.

We do not have to strain our ears today to hear the dripping water of people washing their hands in Pilate's bowl: "I don't like this racial discrimination or segregation. But what can I do? It isn't my fault. My hands are clean." "Sure, some legislation smells to heaven. It is treason to all that has been best in American history. But I didn't write it. It isn't my fault."

Please pass the washbowl!

Yours,

SIMEON STYLITES.

The Pastor in Greek Mythology

Sir: The pastor of St. John's-by-the-Gas-Station was dining on Grilled American at the drugstore counter. He looked up sadly as I joined him. "I've just discovered another ancestor," he said, "my real spiritual ancestor. Tithonus. You know — the old boy in Greek mythology who was changed by a girl named Aurora into a grasshopper. That is what I am. And a lot of other parsons. We have been changed into grasshoppers. Look out!" And he vaulted from the stool into a Community Chest luncheon ten blocks away.

I think he really had something. A good many modern pastors have ancestors in Greek mythology. There is the Rev. Dr. Tithonus, for one. At times he seems like the community grasshopper, leaping wildly from spot to spot, the nearest thing to perpetual motion yet achieved. He even telephones in his sleep. His sad condition is like that of the busy man whose secretary left on his desk a telephone directory with the notation, "These people called you." I do not know whether grasshoppers ever rest or hibernate or not. Probably, like old soldiers, they just fade away. For Dr. Tithonus' sake, I hope there are no luncheon meetings, committee meetings, or campaigns in heaven.

Then there is Sisyphus. He was a king of Corinth who was condemned to roll a big stone up a hill, only to have it always roll down again as soon as it reached the top. What parish parson has not thought of Sisyphus as bone of his bone and flesh of his flesh? He rolls a heavy stone — that is, the whole parish — up to the top on Sunday morning, when, plunk! Monday finds it rolled down again. Lent culminates in Easter, with even the local Century Plants, in the front row, flowering in new millinery. But the day after another enormous heave to the top is called for. No wonder so many chaplains found the transfer from the army or navy back to the parish difficult. They learned, what a man in the military chaplaincy may forget, that any voluntary organization may start slipping downhill next Wednesday.

Then there is Cyclops, the one-eyed wonder. Who does not know the Rev. Mr. Cyclops, the man with one eye and one idea, who sees life steadily and sees it all wrong? The Roman Cato was a Cyclops, with one burning eye — "Carthage must be destroyed." What the one eye sees varies with the times. A hundred years ago, Brother Cyclops had as the third point of every sermon, infant baptism—either for or against, with vehemence. Now he camps on one or other of any number of things, according to his choice. But he sees it with one eye only. There is the near-psychologist Cyclops with his reiterated message, "You, too, can be a Booming Success, like Me," and there is the Rev. Karl (either Marx or Barth) Cyclops with single vision fixed on a single point.

At the other extreme there is the modern counterpart of Argus, the lad with a hundred eyes. He sees so many things simultaneously that he never sees any of them sharply. In his discourses he considers all things at once and "takes them up in that order." His orations are a pack of firecrackers — lots of noise but not much direction.

The best of the old Greek boys — and thank heaven, he has a host of descendants — was Antaeus. He grew strong whenever his feet touched the ground.

The present-day Antaeus has the strength of ten when his feet touch the ground, the very plot of earth on which his hearers live, the problems they have to deal with. Long may he wave!

Yours,

SIMEON STYLITES.

"A Screech of Some Kind"

Sir: My heart leaped up when I beheld, leafing not long ago through Bryce's *The American Commonwealth,* this comment on William James's philosophy: "It is a perfect bog of reasonableness . . . One fairly longs for a screech of some kind." I cannot remember James well enough to know whether that comment is justified, though I know more of him than of any other philosopher, he being the only one of that ilk that I was ever able to understand even partially. (Yes, I know philosophers do not write for minds like mine.) But Bryce's remark set me to thinking about many things where a screech of some kind is called for.

It sometimes applies to the radio. Often in the evening hours when I am overwhelmed with the smooth, soporific perfection of a mellifluous voice announcing that "more people smoke Camels than ever before," I can understand why many listeners prefer the dissonances of Jimmy Durante or the breathless bombardment of Walter Winchell. They are at least human noises.

I long for a screech of some kind in many addresses, in the pulpit or otherwise. There is so much lucid statement and perfect taste on many a wild and whirling occasion that calls for something more primitive and damaging. So many sermons are like the description given by a disillusioned author of writing a book: "It's like dropping a rose leaf down the Grand Canyon and waiting to hear the echo." Lots of homilies are rose leaves dropping with no detonation. Ezekiel had a word for it: "For, lo, thou art to them as a very lovely song of one that hath a pleasant voice . . . for they hear thy words, but do them not."

There is a tradition in a middle western college that the chapel building once caught on fire (not, I regret to say, from a sermon), and a mild-mannered secretary stepped apologetically into the chaplain's office on the first floor and whispered, "I am awfully sorry to disturb you, but I think the building is on fire." I have heard a good many sermons like that. Of course a screech will not put out a fire, but it might pave the way for action. A screech is not a means of salvation, but it might lead to the preliminary — conviction of sin. At least, it might be more fitting than an expostulation like Moses' mother's in the old jingle:

Once there was a boy named Moses
Who cut off both his sisters' noses.
That made them look so very queer
That mother said, "Why, Moses dear!"

A "perfect bog of reasonableness' is quicksand for the gospel. Deep bottom is pictured by Dickens in *Edwin Drood,* where a minister says, "Keeping our hearts warm and our heads cool, we clergy need do nothing emphatically."

The rebuttal to this, of course, is that anything like a screech is emotional, disorderly, and extreme. Exactly! Those are the three indelible marks of New Testament Christianity. Read the book some time and see if this is not so.

A fire engine just went by. I may be mistaken, but it didn't seem to me that the sirens were playing "God bless America." Instead, it sounded definitely like a screech of some kind.

Yours,

SIMEON STYLITES.

The Hour-a-Day Work Week

Sir: A candidate for Member of Parliament in Great Britain, not long ago, ran on an unusual platform. Alas, he was defeated! The defeated candidate was Alexander Hancock, a retired shoe manufacturer, who ran on a platform calling for "a one-hour-a-day work week," which he practices, so he said, himself. There, my masters, is a Statesman, a man after my own heart, a man of vision and genius. I had the idea before he did.

That is the way I long have sought,
And mourned because I found it not.

I wish Mr. Hancock might have had a chance to put this liberating idea on the statute books.

I have always encountered a miserable, obscurantist prejudice in favor of an eight- or twelve-hour day. The butcher, the baker, and the candlestick maker (that is, the United Illuminating Co.) have always compelled me to work, if not from early dawn, at least too long, so that my spirits become soggy by 10 a.m. Even then I cannot make both ends meat, so one has to be carrots. It is an imperfect world.

But there is a silver lining, which I point out to you. If you have to work eight hours a day for slave drivers, you can work one hour a day for yourself. When you leave the slave pen you can have one "crowded hour of glorious life" doing something that does not make sense, except that you want to do it. If that isn't good sense, what is?

Some of your readers may get a new outlook on life from this. For perhaps I am not the only complete nitwit who reads your paper. In fact, as I look over your correspondence columns I feel that that is a reasonable possibility.

There are two inexorable conditions to be observed. One, the work must have no financial return or value at all. Two, there must be no conceivable point at which it would be of any use to anyone. Stick to those two rules and you can have a whale of a time.

For instance, a block away lives a bookkeeper who gives an hour a day to the art of the flute. Oft in the stilly night — or it was still until he began — with his weird notes there comes to mind a text from the Bible, "O Lord, how long!" Then I think of a more fitting text: "Life is more than meat, and the flute than a double-entry ledger." The man at the filling station is writing a novel in his hour a day working for himself alone. He has not let me see it. I suspect the casualty rate in it is high. I know that there is not a drop of gasoline in the five hundred pages already done. I am acquainted with a manufacturer who does needlepoint. He has covered a pillow with it. The stitches are either Surrealist or Dada, but they brought him freedom of soul.

For myself, I would like to take up carving little ships in bottles. But such things are too high for me, I cannot attain to them. So I guess my hour a day will have to be given to restoring antiques, including

Yours,

SIMEON STYLITES.

"Know-How"

Sir: I am a charter member of a new society organized to eliminate a verbal abomination from our common speech — the alleged word "know-how." Will you join our little group?

I am sick of "know-how." You can hardly read a

column in a newspaper or a page in a magazine without running smack into it. We are reassured about the Russians because "they haven't got the *know-how* to run up a stockpile of atomic bombs as high as the Washington monument." Or, "American industry is bound to dominate the world because we have the *know-how.*"

The word is a counterfeit. It is debasing the currency of the English language — one of those hyphenated frauds which are not words at all but lazy substitutes for precision of diction, which are increasingly on the tongue and, I fear, will eventually get into the dictionary.

Worse than that, the word — to call it that — is a perfect symbol of what is the matter with us and has been the matter with us for a long time. In brief, it expresses the fatal confusion of technical skill, baptized complacently and conceitedly as the "know-how," with wisdom about life. We give so much attention to the "know *how,*" so little to the "know *what.*" We take an adolescent delight in tools and have little mature insight into what to do with them.

The word and its unending use conceal a truth that ought not to be concealed; that is, that we do not really know more about life and its major issues, about goodness and beauty, than our fathers did, but merely have more things to befuddle us and cover over our lack of knowledge. Many of our contemporaries fall into a tragic mistake about the calendar. They make it the measure of all things, the determiner of value, with which, of course, it has nothing to do. The infantile syllogism runs something like this: Plato and Jesus and Thomas Jefferson never rode in a jet-propelled plane; consequently their ideas are all out of date.

This genuflection before the "know-how" is the dominant note in the many surveys of the years 1900–1957 that have been filling the papers and magazines. We know more than our fathers and mothers of 1900 because, poor simpletons, they didn't have the "know-how." So we look with a complacent smirk at the automobiles of 1900, the one lung chuggers; at the crazy kite the Wright brothers flew at Kitty Hawk; at the first crude movie peep shows; and at the wall telephones with little cranks to grind. And we chant, Verily we are the people, for if wisdom did not begin with us it certainly ends with us. (Which is a far more subtle and dangerous arrogance than that pilloried in Job, which declared, wisdom shall die with us.)

We look back in amazement at the "pill era" in medicine, when most of the public was sure that there was an infallible pill for every ailment, from pallid cheeks to cancer. But we have its equivalent — the abiding faith of millions that there is, or soon will be, a gadget for every need. Depression coming? Cheer up! There will be a new gadget to save us. Remember the automobile! War in the offing? Don't worry! There will be a new gadget which will make the old blockbuster look like a blank cartridge, and our side will have it. We have the "know-how"! Boredom a danger? Don't be silly! There will be a new gadget to take care of all that! Life can be beautiful at $249 a set, easy payments.

We turn our back on the wisdom of the Old Testament, which points out the folly of making the means of production — the net and the drag — an idol; and on the wisdom of Jesus, who shows us the fatal mistake of preoccupation with means rather than ends. That fellow who pulled down his barns — he had the "know-how" to build bigger and better grain elevators . . . and stomach ulcers.

Our generation has experimented long enough with trying to make the laboratory a temple for the human spirit. The laboratory is too small. Even Einstein's 1950 gift to the world — a new equation for gravitation — will not serve as a foundation for man's deepest hopes.

That is one reason why I think the church had better stick around. For in a world filled with so much pagan worship of "know-how," it has an imperishable word on what to know.

Yours,

SIMEON STYLITES.

The Big Bores

Sir: Believe it or not — and you won't — the publishing journals have announced a volume with this title: *Practical Dope on the Big Bores,* by F. C. Ness, published by Stackpole & Heck. I hurried to get a copy and, after clearing many hurdles, finally did, only to be greatly disappointed. I turned to the index and ran down the S's, looking for "Stylites, Simeon," to see how my pedigree would look in print. The name wasn't there at all. Imagine a book on bores that omitted Simeon! Stranger still, I looked up some of my best friends, and they weren't listed either. A very superficial volume!

Then I looked at the title page and discovered that it was a book on guns, about "large style cartridges developed during the last twenty years."

There ought to be a directory of the more familiar kind of bores, orators, and raconteurs and suchlike. It is an alluring subject.

Of course, the biggest bore is the person who is always making lists of bores and calling other people bores. That covers my case nicely. We all know, by tutelage of Dr. Freud, that such an affliction is just a case of suppressed jealousy, the people who are bores themselves imputing a gift for inducing yawns to other people.

Now that that is out of the way, consider two genuine blown-in-the-bottle bores, be their habitat the platform or the living room.

The Oscar for the finest performance goes to the person who can never really give himself up to a subject in meandering talk and lose himself in it. No matter what the subject of conversation, whether the future of the United Nations or when to plant Kentucky Wonders, this sixteen-inch bore always has himself in the wings, waiting for a cue to come on the stage and do an exhibitionistic dance. When he doesn't hear any cue, he rushes in anyway.

If his neighbor timidly suggests that perhaps we may not have a war with Russia, he plumps in with, "I was talking just last year about that with Winston Churchill. I said to him, 'Winnie, what do you think?' He put his arm around my neck and said, 'George' — he always calls me George — 'I have wanted to ask you that. Your experience is so much greater than mine' . . ." (twenty-minute blackout.) Thus the music of real talk is interrupted by a "commercial" advertising himself.

Of lesser bore, but still a devastating killjoy, is the person of such painful simplicity that he has one panacea for all ills and rubs it into every patient or audience. He is integrated to a terrifying degree. All conversational roads lead to the same Rome — his, or her (don't forget the ladies!), pet solution for what ails us, whether it be communism, world government, or the ten-day reducing diet. The theme song is always the same:

After careful meditation,
And profound deliberation,
On the various petty projects which have been shown,
Not a scheme in agitation,

For the world's amelioration,
Has a grain of common sense in it except my own.

Yours,

SIMEON STYLITES.

Assets of Doubtful Value

Sir: Some days ago I was looking over the report of the treasurer of a large institution of great social usefulness. In the midst of pages of figures and magic symbols, such as A.T.&T., A.T.&S.F., C.B.&Q., $82,746, I came across a mournful page that was almost completely blank. At the top was a solitary entry:

Assets of Doubtful Value $1.00

Perhaps a good many people have such a sad page in their financial records:

100 shares of The Holding Company That
Let Go $1.00

Then my mind bounced clear off the page to a lot of other alleged assets of supposedly great worth which are of decidedly doubtful value when the books are balanced. Dr. Wallace Petty, of blessed memory, used to tell of a chest of silver that was given to him and his wife in an early parish. It was a beautiful, costly possession and the pride of their lives. They took good care of it. Every night they carried it upstairs and every morning they carried it downstairs again.

Every summer when they went away, even for only a week, they made a trip to the safety deposit vault and left it there, and when they returned made another trip to retrieve it.

Finally they discovered that they had become nursemaids to a chest of silver, and they made a declaration of independence. They left the chest downstairs one night, and a note on the dining-room table, which read, "Dear Burglar, The silver is in the sideboard." And they lived happily ever after. The pride of their lives had become a doubtful asset.

This theme, of course, is a natural for sour grapes. It is easy to pretend that anything we do not have is of doubtful value. The noble and shining army of the bald-headed assert that heavy black hair is an asset of doubtful worth. Think of the time wasted in brushing it, three times a day, 365 days a year! Also, the bald-headed never have to worry about getting gray!

But not all grapes are sour. For instance, there are talents of various sorts, parlor tricks of many kinds, all the way from playing a violin like Kreisler to reciting "Curfew Shall Not Ring Tonight." They look like wonderful assets, and cause ungifted souls to sink into melancholia. But the result of possessing them is often that a man does the parlor trick rather than his main job. It was a wise mother who said to her daughter, "My dear, we know you are not pretty, so you had better be smart." Many a preacher to whom some wicked fairy gave at birth a wonderful singing voice or a flair for dramatic recitals would be far better off if he had nothing to rely on but making good at his chief job.

Money can be and has been an asset of very doubtful value. And no sour grapes about it either. The lack of money has compelled people to extend themselves. It is not cynicism that sees that much of the best work ever done has been done because someone was "broke." Some of the finest literature ever written was written with the bill collector sitting on the doorstep. (I have discovered, however, that it takes more than the bill collector to insure the production of good literature.)

This ought to end here, for this paragraph will cost me my friends, all three of them. But something else occurs to me. A former neighbor of mine, who is now president of a college, told me the other day (after swearing me to secrecy) that he thought the Ph.D. degree was a very doubtful asset for teaching. And that is not sour grapes, for he has one out of the top drawer. He thinks the Ph.D. has become a fetish, a form of idolatry, which has small relation to good teaching. He quoted some iconoclast who said that the average Ph.D. thesis is just "moving bones from one graveyard to another." Ten thousand freshmen know that the poorest teaching in the United States is being done by young Ph.D.'s who have never given ten minutes in their lives to learning how to teach and who regard classes as complete bores.

Perhaps some day colleges will stop worshiping idols and start training teachers. Hope springs eternal in the breast of

Yours,

SIMEON STYLITES.

Consider the Corncrake

Sir: I try to learn something new every year. I do not always make it, but this year I have already learned something, and the year is not yet half over. I have learned what a corncrake is. I always thought it was some sort of harvesting machine that went up and down the rows of corn and picked off the ears. Now I have learned that it is a bird. The dictionary calls it "a European rail," and adds that it is a bird common in grain fields.

I began my researches on the corncrake through coming across a tribute to its noble qualities paid about a century ago by Dean Liddon of St. Paul's Cathedral in London. The dean's friend, Dr. T. B. Strong, bishop of Oxford, tells us about it:

> We were walking in the fields and heard a corncrake croaking in the grass.
>
> "I like that bird," Liddon said. I said I thought I had heard birds that sang better.
>
> "Oh, it's not that," said Liddon. "To me it represents moral earnestness. It goes on saying what it knows to be unpalatable."

That is a rare kind of courage — "moral earnestness to keep on saying what it knows to be unpalatable." We need in the United States today the croaking of the corncrake rather than the screaming of the American eagle.

Of course there is no virtue in constantly serving up the unpalatable just for the sake of causing wry faces and sour stomachs. Mere pugnacity gives a stimulation like that of whisky, and is just as deceptive. A single-minded devotion to unpopular truth may be a form of exhibitionism — the only way one can get attention. The English poet Samuel Rogers, who is remembered far more for his breakfast parties than for his poetry, once confessed, "I have a weak voice and unless I say something nasty no one will pay any attention to me."

Nevertheless, the moral earnestness of the corncrake is needed, on the street, in the school, in the legislative halls, and in the pulpit. Truth which has any saving power in a world rushing down a steep place is bound to be unpalatable to large numbers of people and to strongly entrenched interests. Mr. Dooley is a good guide for any public figure. He said, "It is my business to comfort the afflicted and to afflict the comfortable." That, by the way, is a good book on preaching in thirteen words.

We read in the Song of Solomon that "the voice of the turtle [dove] is heard in the land." That is a sign of spring. But internationally and in almost every other way it is still deep winter, and the voice of the corncrake is far more in order than the song of the turtle dove.

The nation needs to hear unpalatable things about our foreign policy. More and more we tend to approach the whole question of world survival with the mind of a drill sergeant. In his introduction to *Androcles and the Lion,* George Bernard Shaw wrote: "The world is largely governed by considerations which occur to stockbrokers in the first five minutes." We are worse off than that. We seem to be governed, in fateful hours, by considerations that occur to generals in the first two minutes, and by little else. One encouraging note is that there has been a decidedly corncrake quality in recent statements by many religious bodies on this danger. Talk about civil liberties is very unpalatable in many places. The one counsel is, "For heaven's sake, drop it." There is need for the continuous, even if raucous, song of the corncrake.

I see I have become quite an ornithologist. Yet I have never seen or heard a corncrake. Will someone please tell me whether it thrives and croaks in the U.S.A.?

Yours,

SIMEON STYLITES.

The Human Face Divine

Sir: In the years preceding the formation of the United Church of Canada a questionnaire was sent to ministers in western Canada asking about conditions there. One question was, "What are the chief obstacles to religion in your community?" A certain pastor replied, feelingly, "The chief obstacles to true religion in our community are whisky and the Methodists." When I recounted that bit of history to a Methodist bishop (he had just finished holding an annual conference) he replied, sadly, "I can see his point."

But the other day I ran into a new theory accounting for the decline of religion. I met the pastor of St. John's-by-the-Gas-Station, looking more faded and withered than the last rose of summer. He couldn't have looked more dejected if he had been hit by a ten-ton truck.

"Have you," he asked gloomily, after I had administered first aid in the form of a beaker of Coca-Cola, "ever reflected seriously on the human face?"

"I have a depressed feeling when shaving and looking in the mirror," I admitted.

"Naturally," he agreed, his spirits picking up with a shot of malice. "But I was thinking of something more general. I was out preaching last night at Petunia Corners. It was a stolid audience with faces starkly glum. The faces in Mrs. Jarley's Wax Works are far more animated and vivacious. I felt as helpless as an early Christian martyr being thrown to the lions. But, alas, they did not eat me and thus put me out of my misery; they just stared. It was a bovine stare. And not from contented cows, either! They looked bored to death.

"I have a new theory for the decline and fall of religion. It is not due to science or communism, but to the faces of the congregation. All too often they congeal the preacher and freeze the genial currents of his soul. We read of Another Preacher that in one place 'he could do no mighty work there because of their unbelief.' But in these latter years the apostles can do no mighty work because of the petrified faces they have to look into. When people in the pews have a look of stolid fortitude, like that of a man in the dentist's chair, that makes void the word of God. It is like the old mythology, where the faces of the Furies froze the beholder. Milton wrote of the 'human face divine,' but then Milton was blind.

"A lot of those folks at Petunia — and there are lots of Petunias — break the Second Commandment every Sunday as they look up at the preacher. They make graven images out of their faces. There is never the faintest suggestion of a smile which might rescue the perishing speaker. Of course in church we do not want a guffaw such as would reward a jokester at an Elks convention. But we might have a movement of good will and intelligence, like the faint ripple of a breeze over a wheat field.

"It says in the Good Book that, when engaged in religious exercises, thou shalt 'anoint thy head and wash thy face.' In the Revised Simeon Version this is translated, 'Anoint your face with a look of interest if possible, and wash the look of dumb resignation from your countenance.'

"People can at least make possible the preaching of the Word by putting heart in the speaker, showing by their faces that he is not addressing stone images in Statuary Hall."

Yours,

SIMEON STYLITES.

She Sits in the Seventh Row

Sir: We have with us today a Guest Artist. I like her, and I like her little piece. So here she is to speak it in person. She lives in Los Angeles and wrote this letter:

> DEAR SIMEON: Can't you do something about preachers who don't speak loud enough for me to hear them? I sit up in the seventh row and I'm not deaf—well, not very deaf, anyhow; I can hear anyone whispering about me clear across a big room. But I wonder if the lungs of a lot of preachers are giving out. The Bible asks, "How can they hear without a preacher?" But I ask, "How can they hear even if they have a preacher, if he mumbles softly, as though he were afraid of waking the baby?" Maybe the preacher just runs out of breath, so that I miss the last words of a sentence, which might have been worth hearing. But I never know. If you can do anything to help me, I'll be much obliged. Yours, ———.

Well, at least, by your courtesy, I can get the floor and make a motion. As a result of this letter I have engaged in some high-powered research, and I discover that the lady who sits in the seventh row has the Good Book on her side.

Time would fail to tell of its exhortations to speak with a loud voice or of the times when the messengers of the Lord spoke in a loud voice. The angels in the book of Revelation, seven or eight of them, always speak with a "loud voice," as in 5:12, "An angel proclaiming with a loud voice." Perhaps they wanted to be heard! The Psalms call continually for a loud voice, as in 98:4, "Make a loud noise and rejoice." There are thirty or forty of these directions. The Psalms do not go in for *pianissimo*. St. Paul, speaking to a cripple, "said with a loud voice, Stand upon thy feet." Perhaps that was one reason why the cripple stood up. I'll bet Paul could be heard beyond the seventh row.

Now, you are muttering, "Do you want yelling?" In the language of Holy Scripture I reply, "God forbid." If a horse is a vain thing for safety, a yell is just as vain for inquiring in the temple. But if I had to choose between a yell and an inaudible mutter — which, again, heaven forbid — I would put my money on the yell.

Do you remember the line in Thornton Wilder's play *Our Town* when the leader of the Congregational choir, after hearing them practice, gives a hurt cry, "Leave loudness to the Methodists!" All right, there is no salvation in loudness. But perhaps even the Methodists are having throat or lung trouble these days. (Note to the FBI: What became of all the "shouting Methodists"? I haven't heard one in a long spell.)

The lady in Los Angeles has one point on which many of us might come forward for prayers and say, "God have mercy on me, a sinner." That point is about the voice that runs out of gas. The preacher is reaching a climax. "There is one thing," he cries, "that must never be forgotten, since the most important thing of all is . . . gurgle . . . ugh . . . gurgle" — all lost like the sputter of an idea going down for the third time.

We live in a day when a plane can outrun the sound of a voice. Perhaps we had better step up the voice. Besides, the folks are not all up in the seventh row. The most unregenerate are back in row twenty, or out in the vestibule.

Yours for bigger and better noises,

SIMEON STYLITES.

Take a Shopping Trip

Sir: My neighbor Mrs. Clerihew (everyone within five miles finally emerges as my neighbor, whether he likes it or not) met me on Main street the other day in front of the Bon Ton Emporium. Her face was beaming like an automobile headlight.

"Oh," she cried, "I've had the most wonderful shopping trip of all my life. It was marvelous!"

I looked at her empty hands and asked, "What did you buy?"

"Nothing!" she answered ecstatically. "That's the whole point. That's what makes it perfect."

Somehow my dim wit missed "the whole point." So she sang on: "I came downtown with ten dollars in my pocketbook. Not much for a binge at the Bon Ton. But here it is, as good as new!" And she showed it to me. There it was, all intact, with the steel engraving of Alexander Hamilton and everything.

"I couldn't get the stuff for the cushions to match our old sofa, and the hats were terrible. So I walked around and looked in a lot of windows and stores, and got all steamed up over the enormous number of things I don't want. A thrill, I'm telling you! That's the way to get a lift from shopping — just look at the things you don't want!

"There was a bag from Cartier's, 'very smart imported black-and-white fabric, lined with black calfskin, with removable gold clip, $150.' I'd rather have my old catchall, a bargain at $3.49, but lined with an occasional dollar bill. Then there was that television set, only $595, easy payments till 1999. I wouldn't take it as a gift. Then there was perfume at $50 a sniff. I don't remember whether it was Christmas Night or Fourth of July Morning. I don't want it!" And she danced along the street.

I tried it. It's a lot of fun, and a big boost to your

morale. I too had an engraved portrait of Alexander Hamilton on a green background. I brought it home, all in one piece. The things I didn't want! There was, as alluringly described, "an exceptionally fine porcelain tureen with cover, made in Berlin *circa* 1760, a bargain at $300." I like our old soup bowl better, *circa* 1929, bought at *circa* $1.14.

Then I saw in a display window "the finest thing on wheels, custom-built limousine, its pulse is your pulse, $9,000 delivered." I first said, "Nonsense! The finest thing on wheels is still a baby carriage." Then I firmly and joyously said: "No! I don't want it. If its pulse is my pulse, I want something less excitable than my pulse when a ten-ton truck heaves in view."

You try it. Sally forth some morning with $6.42 in your pocketbook, and count your many blessings among the things you have no yen for. The world is so full of a number of things we don't want that I'm sure we should all be as happy as kings — were supposed to be before they went out of fashion.

Yours,

SIMEON STYLITES.

John Wesley—Revised

Sir: There is a venerable document — an antique by this date — that you ought to get around to reading some time. It is John Wesley's "Rules for a Preacher's Conduct," which is worth committing to memory by lots of people who are not preachers. Most of it is stern stuff, reminding one of the comment of Huckleberry Finn (or was it Tom Sawyer?) on something he was supposed to read: "The statements is interesting but tough." Here, for instance, is one of Wesley's rules: "Always make out what you have in hand." Just try it!

But John made some glaring mistakes, and I have been divinely commissioned to revise him. He includes two rules:

"Never be unemployed."

"Never be triflingly employed."

I would not presume to make any major correction to such a giant, but I am making a very slight emendation of these two rules — just one word changed. Instead of "*Never* be unemployed" read "*Frequently* be unemployed," and instead of "*Never* be triflingly employed" read "*Frequently* be triflingly employed."

The person who is too busy to loaf is too busy. For the soul is squeezed to death by the vise — spell it "vice" and you will still be correct — of unremitting employment. Rudyard Kipling has much evil laid up against him. In the poem "If" (no longer, thank heaven, a form of parlor entertainment) he wrote:

If you can fill the unforgiving minute
With sixty seconds' worth of distance run . . .
You'll be a man —

or something. That is not true. If you are always running sixty seconds' worth every minute you will soon be a tiresome machine, with all imagination, all sense of wonder and poetry, dead. All truly creative power, which is nourished in leisure, will be gone, and only a busy *body* will be left.

Call that a lazy man's gospel if you wish, but history is on the side of the loafer. Didn't Sir Isaac Newton discover gravitation when he was sitting under an apple tree? He would never have thought of it if he had been busy picking the apples. And didn't Darwin and Alfred Russel Wallace both discover evolution when they were in bed? They would never have done it if they had been dictating letters or running for a train. Down with perpetual industry! We know a theological seminary graduate who took along with him on his honeymoon a copy of Driver's *Introduction to the Old Testament* to make sure that he would never be unemployed.

Now about the solemn-owl advice, "Never be triflingly employed." You can always duck that one by asking, "What is a trifle?" It turns out usually to mean something that has no financial pay-off or does not advance a "career." People who scorn trifling employments usually confuse seriousness with solemnity, and the two are worlds apart.

Wesley would have been a lot happier if he'd had a few trivialities. He did not recognize that Grace Murray was foreordained to be his wife. But courtship is mostly "trivialities," and he was not strong on the trivial. If he had been, he would have escaped marrying the harridan who overtook him. Perhaps in the long run his purgatory was the world's gain. Perhaps he would not have ridden so many thousand miles if he could ever have had a quiet cup of tea at home. Nevertheless, it is the "trivial" employment that puts a person in fighting trim.

Come over some time and play canasta. There is a new cushion in the old reclining chair.

Lazily,

SIMEON STYLITES.

On the Surface

Sir: I came across something the other day that has almost made me a Devil's Advocate for one of the most damning adjectives in the English language. I am making my plea in court to see if I can establish a case for the despised adjective "superficial." In the bright lexicon of invective, so volubly used today, there is only one worse word that you can hurl at a person. This is, of course, "optimist." In these dark days an optimist is a little lower than a moron, and is crowned with a complete lack of glory and much dishonor.

The word "superficial" — rightly — carries an aura of disdain. It describes a person who lives "on the surface," who never gets down to the deeper truths and experiences of life. In that sense, of course, to live on the surface of life is to miss life itself, in its large potentialities. The classic picture of a thin life on the surface is in unforgettable words: "Some fell on stony places, where they had not much earth; and forthwith they sprung up, because they had no deepness of earth; and when the sun was up, they were scorched; and because they had no root, they withered away."

Granted. But there is another sense of the words "the surface of life" in which "superficiality" can be a great resource for richness of experience and recurring happiness. Here is E. F. Benson, in his memoirs, *Final Edition,* describing Lady Sandhurst, a daughter of Matthew Arnold:

> The surface of life never lost its brightness for her. She had her share of sorrows . . . But she found "treats" everywhere, small entrancing surprises: the conduct of the ducks on the Serpentine, when she took walks in Hyde Park; a barrel organ of the old type, with one leg and a red-coated monkey sitting on top, huskily performing "The Lost Chord"; the changing of the guard at Buckingham Palace; the changing of traffic lights, then a new institution; the passing of an aeroplane. . . . She had the genuine Jane Austen eye. Whether she directed it to barrel organs or bombs, she saw with that uniquely humorous perception.

Doesn't that read like an invitation to the dance, a parade of fleeting joys to be found on the surface of the good earth?

I remember an advertisement for some kind of wax or polish of which the slogan was, "Save the surface and you save all." (It was accompanied by a picture of a man pouring boiling water on the gleaming surface of the dining room table. That was a subversive picture: it lured too many excitable youngsters into trying the experiment.) Save the surface of life and you do *not* save all. But you save plenty. The little things that do not plumb the depths of any cosmic issues, that leave life's major problems just as they are — these do not change outward circumstances, but they do change people. A habit of seeing them, of giving oneself up to them when they appear, will keep life from becoming a tiresome game of blindman's buff, blind to the shining surface of life. Blindman's buff is a poor game compared to "I Spy." Spell it "Eye Spy" and you will still be correct. So much of true poetry is the record of a lively game of "I Spy" played on the surface of the earth.

Make your own list of "small, entrancing surprises." Many of the things you choose will be on the list drawn up by anyone with good vision — the shine of streets in the rain at night, wood-smoke, blossoms, the sound of crunching autumn leaves under foot, the feel of kitten's fur. Let me put on the stand two witnesses for the defense. Oliver St. John Gogarty:

> *What can we say but, "Glory be!"*
> *When God breaks out in an apple tree?*

And Ralph Waldo Emerson:

If you do not quit the high chair, lie down and roll on the ground a great deal, you become nervous and heavyhearted. There is health in table talk and nursery play. You must wear old shoes and have aunts and cousins.

There is a higher authority for paying attention to the surface. One great difference between the Synoptic Gospels and the Gospel of John is, quite literally, on the surface. In the Synoptics there is so much of the bright surface of the earth and life on it. Lilies in bloom, a sower striding across the field, a flock of sheep, and homely things such as the mending and re-mending of clothes, the noisy tumult of a wedding, the baking of bread — all these caught His large and luminous eye.

The defense rests.

Yours,

SIMEON STYLITES.

"I Wanted To Go Home"

Sir: It is pretty late to be bringing out any more laurel wreaths for Robert Frost. At the age of eighty plus he has pulled up with all the prizes there are — Pulitzer and Poetry Society awards; in fact, everything except the medal for the Four-Minute Mile. But at least it is in order to offer a few bay leaves for a marvelous word which he spoke at the party honoring him on his eightieth birthday a few years ago. He said he remembered that a delegation once called upon him to inquire into the hidden meanings of some famous lines of "Stopping by Woods on a Snowy Evening." The lines are:

But I have promises to keep,
And miles to go before I sleep.

The delegation asked, "What was the symbol and what were the mystic overtones?"

"All that it means," Mr. Frost replied with a smile, "is that I wanted to go home."

O, wise young man, we thank thee for that word! In these days of symbolism and hidden meanings, when a host of literary critics are running around with Geiger counters trying to detect esoteric, enigmatic meanings where there are none, Mr. Frost's word comes like an acute attack of common sense. His statement that all that the lines meant was the obvious meaning that he wanted to go home resembles the attack of good sense which a Hollywood producer suffered many years ago. The script called for the sound of water running over a board, but after trying everything they could think of, the sound-effects men had to admit the result was far from perfect. Finally the producer came up with a wild, fantastic suggestion: "Why not try water running over a board?" They were desperate, so they were willing to try anything, and it worked!

An explanation such as Frost's takes courage, for

the most disastrous conclusion a critic can come to is that the usual view is the right one. Chesterton writes of that "last and most desperate kind of courage which will induce a man to shout from the housetops that two and two make four." What a critic Frost would have made! So different from the erudite specialists who bring every explanation of a piece of literature except the simple, obvious one. They have changed poetry from something enjoyable to read into a crossword puzzle to be solved only with blood, sweat, and tears.

To some such scholars, Shakespeare is no longer a dramatist; he was a psychoanalyst. Here is one critic taking Hamlet apart: "He had a broken mother tie, a suppressed father fixation, erotic ambivalence, hidden gynephobia, and a huge frustration complex." Put him in a strait jacket and try shock treatment! But once Frost's example is followed a novel may again become a novel and not an allegory depicting an existentialist view of the human dichotomy. Then perhaps people who like a story will not have to fly for refuge to the comics or the Lone Ranger.

And what a biblical critic Frost would have made! Who can compute the weary hours wasted by biblical critics seeking out tortuous meanings to displace simple, obvious ones. There is the verse, "It is easier for a camel to go through the eye of a needle than for a rich man to enter the kingdom of heaven." What weird "explanations" have been given for that, all the way from saying that one of the gates to

Jerusalem was the "needle gate" to things even more ridiculous. Thank God for the scholars who ventured, "Perhaps it means what it says, 'the eye of a needle.' Jesus was indulging in some humorous exaggeration." We hereby nominate Robert Frost for the next vacant Chair of Biblical Exegesis.

Yours,

SIMEON STYLITES.

Salute to Librarians

Sir: Editors know everything. So please tell me who invented the idea of "un-birthday presents." It sounds like *Alice in Wonderland.* Or Robert Louis Stevenson. At any rate it is a good idea. And so, because this is un-National Librarians Week, we hasten to celebrate and raise a paean of gratitude and praise to all librarians, boys and girls, tall and short, stout and slim.

This letter is in three parts: genuflection, hat raising, and lighting a candle, all richly deserved by the profession than whom there is none whicher. We make a genuflection to one of the most missionary-minded collections of people on earth. There is more joy in a librarian's heart over one low-brow infected with the love of reading than there is over four dozen professors with brief cases. Whenever a librarian finds someone looking for a book other than the best-seller just laid that morning, the frenzy of joy bursts forth and the lucky borrower can have the whole stack.

So we genuflect and hold hats high, for the librarian has a whole fleet of magic carpets, which he floats up to your door, all ready to take you to faëry lands forlorn or to Samarkand, Cathay, and way stations. Let him — it is usually her — arrange your itinerary across the seas and the centuries and you can really say, "Much have I traveled in the realms of gold."

Not long ago a librarian in Philadelphia had to write his occupation in his income tax report. He wrote, "Traffic Officer." A friend said, "You cheerful liar! When were you a traffic officer?" He said "All the time. Traffic officers usually prevent collisions. I have been arranging collisions, productive collisions between people and ideas. That's what a book is at its best, a collision. Once in a while I pull off a beaut."

The librarian has to take part of his pay, alas, in spiritual currency. Yet he has his rewards. The most exciting and best reward is that reported by Samuel Gridley Howe, speaking of his education of the little blind, deaf, and dumb girl who preceded Helen Keller. Dr. Howe said, "I fished for many months without any bite at all. Then there was a nibble, then a tug, and up came the soul of Laura Bridgman." Good fishing! So the modern Izaak Walton, or Rebecca Walton, the librarian of the Paradise Branch of the Public Library, baits the hook with the right book — a job calling for rare skill — and casts. And then a little nibble, then a tug, and up comes the soul! It's a better sport than trout fishing.

So, in the immortal language of Sophie Tucker, "Give this little girl a great big hand!"

Vociferously,

SIMEON STYLITES.

Consider the Duck

Sir: Can you tell me whether the duck has ever been used as a Christian symbol? If not, I hereby nominate him for a stained-glass window somewhere.

I have been looking through all the books of religious symbolism I can lay hands on, and am getting quite a collection of animals. The birds rank high. We see the eagle most frequently, holding up the Bible on the lectern with his sturdy wings. Then there is the dove, and even the pelican. I often wonder, Why not the penguin? He is certainly the most ecclesiastical-looking bird of all, arrayed in gown and stole. Every penguin I have ever seen looked exactly like an Archbishop of Canterbury in solemn processional.

Then, of course, there is the lamb, and by grace of Isaiah the lion too has made his way into Christian symbolism.

The case for the duck as a symbol of religion has been beautifully and powerfully portrayed by Donald Babcock in a poem entitled "The Little Duck." * It

* Reprinted, by permission, from the poem *"The Little Duck"* by Donald Babcock; Copr. 1947 The New Yorker Magazine, Inc.

deserves remembrance for its sure insight. Here are the two concluding stanzas:

Now we are ready to look at something special.
It is a duck riding the ocean a hundred feet beyond the surf.
No, it isn't a gull,
A gull always has a raucous touch about him.
This is some sort of a duck and he cuddles in the swells;
He isn't cold, and he is thinking things over.
There is a big heaving in the Atlantic, and he is a part of it.

He looks a bit like a mandarin, or the Lord Buddha, meditating under the Bo tree.
But he has hardly enough above the eyes to be a philosopher.
He has poise, however, which is what a philosopher must have.
He can rest while the Atlantic heaves, because he rests in the Atlantic.

Probably he doesn't know how large the Atlantic is.
And neither do you.
But he realizes it.
And what does he do, I ask you? He sits down in it.
He reposes in the immediate, as if it were infinity — which it is.
That is religion, and the duck has it.
He has made himself part of the boundless, by easing himself into it just where it touches him.

I like the little duck.
He doesn't know much.
But he has religion.

Perhaps that is religion, pure and undefiled — sitting down in the Atlantic ocean without fear or flurry, "making himself part of the boundless, by easing himself into it just where it touches him." That has been done by people as well as by ducks. It is a concrete picture of familiar words: "In Whom we live, and move, and have our being."

In view of this I have a new project. I am going to see if I cannot persuade some church to put in a new stained-glass window, one in which the sunshine will light up a serene little duck riding the waves.

Yours,

SIMEON STYLITES.

Red Ink

Sir: A cynical economist has predicted for the coming year a rising market for red ink. He says there will be a lot of use for it in entering items in the deficiency columns in our budget books. (I am afraid he is right. My bank has a bottle of red ink. They used it on my last statement.)

But I have got off the track. What I started out to tell you was to be sure to have some red ink handy and use it to write up the red-letter events that may get by you if you don't mark them with a sort of festival illumination.

Here is a man who made good use of red ink in writing his voluminous journals — Bronson Alcott. He was a complete flop at making a living and a complete success at making a life. He wrote up the important events in red ink — the birth of his daughters, his first reading of Plato, the first robin in spring, the color of the Concord trees in the fall — the *big* things.

We have too few extra-illuminated pages in our book of life. Take a leaf out of Alcott's journals and write a few more red exclamation points of your own. It will make your days more like the unfolding of an exciting mystery story and less like a Sears-Roebuck catalogue.

The possible harvest of the eye deserves red ink more often than we use it. It was a wise man who said that the last judgment he feared was standing before a great white throne and hearing a voice ask, "Well, what did you think of my world?" and his having to answer, "I didn't really see it. I was busy telephoning."

Every new mechanical gadget deepens the necessity for training ourselves and our children to experience the joys and excitements of the visible world. Otherwise, we shall be, as the headmaster of Harrow predicted, like Plato's company of people, sitting in a dark cave looking at shadows and never seeing the real world. Come to think of it, a company of people sitting in a room gazing at a television set may come pretty close to Plato's prisoners in a cave watching flickering shadows.

Here is a man at work writing up big events in red ink:

And whoever wakes in England
Sees, some morning, unaware,
That the lowest boughs and the brush-wood sheaf
Round the elm-tree bole are in tiny leaf,
While the chaffinch sings on the orchard bough
In England — now!

Here is an earlier entry: "Consider the lilies, how they grow."

Red ink is also called for when we first collide with a real idea. Once there was a man who died at twenty-eight after having been "broke" all his life. But he had a grand collision in his mind, of which he wrote a report in red ink:

Then felt I like some watcher in the skies
When a new planet swims into his ken.

Yours,

SIMEON STYLITES.

I Am Elected Secretary

Sir: I am sorry to have to report that a few days ago someone beat me to the draw. No blood was shed.

No shots were fired. But the other man drew first. I know I would not last long in a mining camp.

I was in a meeting of a fair-sized committee and some real discussion was going on. I was quite steamed up about it, even to the extent of making a fiery speech (that is, of course, fiery for me), complete with two gestures, one with a clenched fist indicating defiance. Then, suddenly, the secretary was called away, and before I could nominate the man sitting next to me to take his place, he nominated me. And all the people who did not want to be secretary voted for me, and I was elected unanimously — the only time in my life that anything like that ever happened.

I was astonished at the change that came over me. I went into the usual secretarial coma. I was so oppressed with the responsibility of getting it all down — who did what — that all interest in the subject of the debate was completely blotted out. I was like the man in Bret Harte's "The Society upon the Stanislaus," who was hit by a rock in the stomach, whereupon

He smiled a kind of sickly smile and curled up on the floor,
And the subsequent proceedings interested him no more.

At least, the subsequent proceedings did not interest me except to get them in the minutes. Was that a substitute or an amendment? What was the motion before the house, if any? My kingdom for a Robert's Rules of Order!

I have since wondered if that is what happens to secretaries. Do they, as a class, get so lost in the records that the real subject is eclipsed? Does the means blot out the end?

It certainly happens in education. To many an administrator the job of keeping the educational system going is so demanding that there is little or no time, strength or interest left for education. Large systems and institutions work automatically toward the isolation of the administration. So we have our school system often directed from downtown offices by people who have not stepped into a classroom in twenty years. Bliss Perry once said in crossing Harvard Yard, "I feel as though I were going through a cemetery, for there are teachers buried under those rolltop desks."

Perhaps one trouble with institutions, including the church, is that they have been so largely directed by men with secretarial minds, concerned with mechanisms and means rather than with experiments and ends. It does not always happen, of course. Some of the most prophetic voices in America have been those of board secretaries. Bishops have been prophets, and many of them are still living, thank God. But there is always the lurking danger of intellectual and spiritual coma brought on by keeping the minutes in order.

If you ever feel the secretarial seizure coming on, throw the minutes in the wastebasket and say your piece on the main subject (if you can remember what it is). You will be out of order. But so were Amos, Luther, and William Lloyd Garrison.

Yours,

SIMEON STYLITES.

The Church of St. Demas

Sir: Perhaps it was only in a nightmare, but I have a sharp remembrance of seeing a church with an unfamiliar name, the Church of St. Demas. It was a beautiful structure, set well back from the street behind a spacious lawn — an ideal church.

I was greatly surprised to read the name, St. Demas. But why not? Nearly every other character mentioned in the New Testament has a church named after him. All the twelve disciples, except Judas. Most of the people in the book of Acts, except Ananias, the liar. And many of the people in the Epistles. Except one, and he well deserves a church — the one with the moving description in the Epistle to the Romans, "Quartus, a brother." That is all. But that is plenty! Even I would like to join a Church of St. Quartus.

But there I go on a detour again. To get back to Demas. He was the disciple immortalized, you remember, in II Timothy: "Demas hath forsaken me, having loved this present world." Perhaps that designation for a church came from a burst of penitential frankness; perhaps from a sense of remarkable fitness. At any rate, there it was, St. Demas.

The mark of a Church of St. Demas would be a love

of this present world, a love so appreciative and so deep that it would not want to antagonize this present world to any degree. St. Demas' pulpit is careful in its choice of themes. In that it resembles some types of journalism, recently described by a distinguished journalist in these vivid words:

> "Afghanistanism" is a word coined to cover editorial preoccupation with distant matters, while local affairs are disregarded. It is nothing new. When I was the youngest reporter on my first job the oldest editor had the name of "Aguinaldo" Haywood. He won it just after the Spanish-American War. At that time there was a minor Tweed regime down at the courthouse. But Aguinaldo had little to say about the local grafting. However, he was highly indignant over the Filipino guerrilla, who was reluctant to accept America's assumption of the white man's burden. Mr. Haywood gave Aguinaldo hell!

St. Demas' church goes in strongly for Afghanistanism. St. Demas goes in strongly for another country also. That is Palestine. Palestine is such a *safe* country — that is, if care is taken not to let any moral or lesson escape into the U.S.A. and come to rest at Megalopolis or Meadowbrook Corners. The preacher can denounce the Pharisees with no more danger of any modern parallel sticking out than stuck out for the pious lady who said after hearing a blistering sermon on the Pharisees of old, "I'm glad I'm not like those Pharisees!"

Alvin Johnson in his autobiography says that no idea ever kept his interest unless he could do something about it. St. Demas does not go to that extreme. Ideas do not seem to be something to do anything about, just something to listen to for twenty minutes while the choir gets a rest. When a typical member of St. Demas' Church says, "I was deeply moved this morning," he does not mean that he was moved to start a riot or any sanctified indiscretion, but just "moved" to a more comfortable place on the pew cushion.

Yours,

SIMEON STYLITES.

"Old Fuss and Feathers"

Sir: Can you tell me offhand who it was that introduced soup into American history? I thought not. It was General Winfield Scott, known to many of his contemporaries and to history as "Old Fuss and Feathers." You have only to look at the photographs of him, all arrayed in full-dress uniform, complete with medals and whiskers, to see how he came by the nickname.

The soup was one of his great achievements. To announce the victory at Vera Cruz in the Mexican war he sent a telegram beginning, "After a hasty plate of soup, I have the honor to announce the capture of Vera Cruz." The plate of soup, in such a connection, rocked the country with delight. The words picture the general's gift for dramatizing himself and usually making himself ridiculous.

General Scott earned his title of "Old Fuss and Feathers" by two things: first, a grandmotherly preoccupation with incidental details and a fidgety worry over them; and second, an inordinate concern over decorations, honors, position, and titles — in other words, feathers. He was so utterly serious and solemn about this that, ironically, it made him a figure of comedy. He raised a bitter diplomatic squabble because the Duke of Wellington was given precedence over him at a state function. True, Wellington was the hero of Waterloo, but Scott was the victor of Lundy's Lane!

General Scott is worth recalling now and then, if only because fuss and feathers are two very real liabilities of life. He becomes a sort of saving mirror in which we can see how we look when we go in for fuss and feathers. Perhaps we can say that they are particularly the dangers of professional life of any sort. A clergyman can easily become a sort of ecclesiastical fuss-box. He deals with so many things, is so greatly concerned that they be done right, that he can lose the sense of proportion. He may get so busy fussing over pigmy events that he has no ammunition left when a major battle comes up.

The concern for "feathers" is a particular danger in those professions where the money reward is not great and the desire for self-assurance takes other forms. "Feathers" include recognitions, titles, posts, decorations — the outside paraphernalia as opposed to inner reality. Minor ceremonials become major passions, such as salutations in the market place and chief seats in the synagogue.

One peacock spreading his feathers was taken down not long ago. A minister was called on the phone and a brisk voice asked, "Is this Mr. Jones?" The minister corrected the speaker gravely: "This is *Doctor* Jones." The man on the phone answered, "This is Bachelor Smith."

Speaking of peacocks, it would be a fine thing if a few of them were on exhibition on the courthouse square in every city, just to remind us all how silly we look when we spread our feathers. Tennyson urged us, you remember, to "let the ape and tiger die." Tough trick to do. But while we are at it it would be a good thing to let the peacock die, too. We all seem to have a peacock, frantically interested in feathers, away back somewhere in our family line, and ready to emerge again at any time.

Yours,

SIMEON STYLITES.

"At Home in Any Cemetery"

Sir: It is an arresting phrase to bump into, that which John Lothrop Motley, the historian of the Dutch Republic, put into a letter home during his researches in Holland. He noted the sharp contrast between his lack of acquaintance and his historical study. He wrote that he did not know many living people but "would feel at home in any cemetery."

That is a vivid way of picturing one's possession of the past. To "feel at home in any cemetery" is one of life's great prizes. More and more people today seem not to be at home in any cemetery. They live in one tense, the present. And life in one dimension takes on a curiously thin quality. So far as their mental and spiritual life is concerned, there was no past. History is what Henry Ford called it, "bunk." A reviewer of Arthur Koestler's novels said of him, "He seems unaware that thought existed before Freud, Marx and Stalin." Whether they are true of Koestler or not, the words are a fair description of the blight of contemporaneousness that has settled on many minds.

Failure to be at home in the cemetery — that is, living without a sense of the past or knowledge of it — brings dire results. For the home of the truly living is in the cemetery. Without familiarity with the past, one has no standards but the trivial ones of the moment. As Mark Pattison wrote, "A man who does not know what has been thought by those who went before him is sure to set an undue value on his own ideas, ideas which have been tried and found wanting." It is the fashion among many today to be so eager to overtake the day after tomorrow that they have no time to catch up with the day before yesterday. "Those who do not know the past are bound to repeat its errors." Thus in religion the stock heresies of fifteen hundred years ago are dusted off and trotted out as the latest advance of truth.

We have many houses in these days of the "latest thing" that have three bathrooms and a rumpus room but no room for a bookcase. Public opinion polls bring little cheer. Dr. Gallup's latest sleuthing reveals that fewer books get read in America than in any other major English-speaking democracy in the world, and that the man in the street in England, who rarely has gone to school beyond his fifteenth year, actually reads more books than people who have attended college in this country. Will this turn out to be, as Irwin Edman feared not the "century of the common man" but of the "commonplace man"?

How much we miss when we are not at home in the cemetery in this sense! Theresa Hooley gives a glimpse of that loss, in a sonnet in the London *Times:*

"A sonnet takes a minute to read," he said.
Spoil of the world in sixty seconds' space!
Milton's illumined blindness; the still face
Of dawn on Westminster Bridge — ecstasy, dread;
Shakespeare's lament for beauty, summer-sped . . .

Compared to this lore of yesterday, how thin the life in one dimension, the cult of the quick summary, the nifty wisecrack, the latest gimmick!

Nothing is more needed in the religious world than to be at home in the cemetery, in the great past of Christian thinking and living. Such an extension of acquaintance will save the church from the calamitous blunder of trading a great heritage of thought for a mess of psychological twaddle hot off the griddle.

Yours,

SIMEON STYLITES.

"Stout Cortez"

Sir: This is a present from John Keats. It ought to be worth a lot to anyone who writes or speaks and has any curiosity about whether anyone is reading or listening. You know they try to find out for the radio how many, if any, are listening to programs — something done with mirrors and telephones and called the "Hooper Rating" or some other kind of rating. But that is very inadequate. The Keats Rating which I am going to give you is a lot more scientific.

You remember that in his sonnet "On First Looking into Chapman's Homer" Keats pulled a gorgeous boner:

> *Or like stout Cortez when with eagle eyes*
> *He stared at the Pacific — and all his men*
> *Looked at each other with a wild surmise —*
> *Silent, upon a peak in Darien.*

There are three schools of thought on that passage. The first insists that Keats did not know that Cortez did not discover the Pacific ocean. The second asserts that he wrote "Cortez" because he needed a two-syllable word instead of one with three syllables. The third maintains — and they are doubtless right — that Keats wanted to know whether he had any readers. When someone would write and tell him what an ignoramus he was not to know that Balboa discovered the Pacific, he would have sure proof that someone had read the poem.

It is a good thing to know. There are speakers (of the vacuum school of oratory) who go on for a long stretch, having a perfectly wonderful time up on the platform all by themselves, without any speculation as to whether anyone is listening or not. Someone ought to write a little piece about a surgeon operating on the brain and being interrupted by a nurse who cries, "Hold everything! The patient is passing out" — or "has passed out." The preacher also operates on the brain. There ought to be an acolyte whose duty it would be to step up when necessary during the sermon and announce that the audience was passing out or had passed out. Then the speaker would know where he was or wasn't, and could revise his strategy accordingly.

The sure way of finding out is to make a beautiful blunder intentionally; that will give you your Keats Rating. If anyone writes in or gives a yell of pain, you will know that you are being read. For instance, in your next editorial on "what to do with Russia," put in the statement, "As Mr. Austin, the former senator from New Hampshire, said the other day . . ." Then when the postman staggers into your office loaded down with letters explaining clearly what an illiterate chump you are for not knowing that Mr. Austin was a senator from Vermont, you will know that you are being read. It's a grand and glorious feeling.

The public speaker has a splendid opportunity to find out whether his audience are listening or whether their fixed attitude of polite attention is the result of their having passed into a coma. Thus, he can quote feelingly, "As Shakespeare says in *Paradise Lost,* 'A man's a man for a' that.' " Of course, some people will not know the difference. But if a dozen persons whisper to him the information that Milton wrote *Paradise Lost* or that Burns wrote "A man's a man," he can lift up his heart with joy. Someone was listening! The preacher can easily find out where he stands by announcing his text as from the first chapter of Revelation, "Now abideth faith, hope and love, these three." If no one makes a protest, he knows he is inside the vacuum.

Philips Brooks, who was for so many years rector of Plymouth Church in Brooklyn, wrote of the loneliness of the preacher who does not know whether his message is being received. Applying this Keats test will cure all that — or leave him in a deeper despair if, as may be the case, he does not hear from a soul.

Another good thing about this test is that when, out of your impressive ignorance, you do make a whopping blunder, you can always say airily, "Why, I just did that on purpose to find out if you were listening." Sometimes you can get away with it.

I dare you to try out your Keats Rating.

Yours,

SIMEON STYLITES.

"Fourscore and Seven Years Ago"

Sir: There are dark moments when the most learned of our philologists incline to the gloomy view that the one universal language, toward which the whole creation moves, will not be Esperanto or English or Eskimo, but Gobbledegook. Some folks, of course, moved by the achievements of our atomic scientists, insist that the one universal language of the not too far future will be the chattering of monkeys in the trees or the buzz of insects hovering above the ruins of a defunct world.

Gobbledegook surely has its chances. It is the official jargon of government agencies and bureaus in all countries. It thrives in a world of "directives," and in the U.S.A. it spreads and kills off the English language as lusty weeds choke off a garden. Many nations claim superiority for their own officialese. But we hope it is not merely nationalistic pride which asserts that the murkiest brand of Goobledegook hails from our own Washington, D.C.

Here is a gaze into the crystal ball of the future, showing what the substitute for the obsolete, old-fashioned English of Shakespeare and Milton and the King James Bible will be, if present trends continue.

Below is an accurate and scholarly translation of Lincoln's Gettsyburg Address into official Gobbledegook. It is the work of Prof. Richard D. Fay of the Massachusetts Institute of Technology, and first appeared in the *Harvard Alumni Bulletin.*

> Eight and seven-tenths decades ago the pioneer workers in this continental area implemented a new group based on an ideology of free boundaries and initial conditions of equality. We are now actively engaged in an over-all evaluation of conflicting factors in order to determine whether or not the life expectancy of this group or of any group operating under the stated conditions is significant. We are met in an area of maximum activity among the conflicting factors. The purpose of the meeting is to assign permanent positions to the units which have been annihilated in the process of attaining a steady state. This procedure represents standard practice at the administrative level. From a more comprehensive viewpoint we cannot assign — we cannot integrate — we cannot implement this area. The courageous units, in being and annihilated, who were active in this area have integrated it to the point where the application of simple arithmetical operations to include our efforts would produce only negligible effects. The reaction of the general public to this colloquium will be nonessential and transitory, but the reaction to the impingement of the

combat group is invariant. It is for this group in being rather to be integrated with the incomplete activities for which the combat groups who were active in this area have so comprehensively effected the initial implementation. It is preferable for this group to be integrated with the incompleted implementation — that from the standards set by these respected deceased units we take accelerated intensive efforts — that we here resolve at a high ethical level that the deceased shall not have been annihilated without furthering the project — that this group under divine leadership shall implement a new source of unhampered activity — and that political supervision composed of the integrated units, for the integrated units, and by the integrated units shall not perish from the superficial area of this planet.

Milton, thou shouldst be living at this hour!

Yours,

SIMEON STYLITES.

The Power of Negative Thinking

Sir: We have heard much in recent days about the Power of Positive Thinking. And we are all for it. It *has* power. We can well call down blessing on each other and intone, "More power to your elbow and to your positive-thinking apparatus."

But we are in danger of much confusion if we are

led to believe that "positive" thinking is the only kind of real value. Too many people today regard "positive thinking" as a form of self-assertion, an act of will, which demonstrates what Powerful Boys and Girls they are. That type is pictured in the classic verses:

There was a young man of Kilpeacon
Whose nose was as red as a beacon.
But by saying "It's white!"
Thirty times, day and night,
He cured it and died an archdeacon.

When positive thinking is identified with a psychological pep talk to oneself, the best things of life and of true growth of mind and heart are left out. We see that in the title of the French translation of one of the most popular of the pep-talk roads to salvation, Dale Carnegie's *Stop Worrying and Start Living.* It came out this way: *"Triomphez de Vos Soucis. Vivez! Que le Diable!"* — which, being interpreted, means: "Overcome your troubles. Live! What the devil!" Just a bit thin!

So in these positive days we may well turn to some pictures of the Power of Negative Thinking, found in an old book that is still read in some quarters — the Bible. The beginning of Christian experience is not in confident self-assertion, but in very negative self-depreciation. The first Beatitude, "Blessed are the poor in spirit, for theirs is the kingdom of heaven," describes the root from which true blessedness grows. The blessed are those who remember their dependence and enter life through the door of humility. That is negative thinking which is the prelude to fruitful living.

We also see the power of very negative thinking about oneself in the words of Peter to Jesus: "Depart from me, for I am a sinful man, O Lord." Again, at the conclusion of the first Christian sermon, men who had been stabbed to the heart by Peter's words asked, "What must we do?" The answer was, in effect, "Do some negative thinking for a change. Repent!"

The power of negative thinking is beautifully and profoundly pictured in the words of the returning Prodigal to his father: "Father, I have sinned against heaven and before you; I am no more worthy to be called your son." That is about as negative as a person can get. And such self-awareness and consciousness of failure is the gateway to power. Humility is the first step in learning.

Such a feeling is very different from the kind of "positive thinking" to which many today are painfully aspiring, the kind that says, "Watch me, boys! I'm going places." That mood may be the beginning of becoming a Big, Booming Success. It is not the door to the life which is Life indeed.

Yours,

SIMEON STYLITES.

Cucumber Sandwich

Sir: Shortly after the close of the First World War a British critic wrote a sharp word about optimistic complacency over world affairs which deserves to be rescued from the limbo of things forgotten. For many people today have entered a lotus land of drugged unconcern. T. E. Hulme wrote: "It is as if you pointed out to an old lady at a garden party that there was an escaped lion twenty yards off, and she was to reply 'Oh yes,' and then quietly take another cucumber sandwich."

Far too many people today are making comments like "Oh yes" and reaching for cucumber sandwiches or something comparable in importance. They have arrived at the stage celebrated by Will Rogers when he said of the easy-going 1920's: "League of Nations? Americans are not bothering about the League of Nations. What they want is some place to park their cars."

Our present plight has much to do with unconcern in the fateful years between the two world wars. We get a clear picture of that unconcern in G. M. Young's biography of Stanley Baldwin, then prime minister of Great Britain. "In some subjects," writes Young, "Baldwin took no interest at all. When the cabinet discussed foreign affairs, he would say, 'Wake me up when you have finished,' and try to get a nap."

In the presence of the atomic threat, too many of us say "Oh yes" and reach for a sandwich. Far too little attention has been given to what may prove to have been the most ominous day in the history of this century — the day last year on which a Japanese sailor died, months after being exposed to the radiation of the hydrogen bomb discharged eighty miles away. For that marked a new epoch in long-range killing, an epoch that cannot be met with a shrug of the shoulders and a sandwich. We are not at a garden party. As Eric Sevareid has commented, "Our time is marked by our impotence to marvel and tremble sustainedly." We can look at the threat of this atomic era, so full of the possibility of annihilation, with our temperature normal. Perhaps a more accurate description would be "subnormal sluggishness." Up to the present time, that has been the attitude of many to the possibilities of the accidental beginning of a third world war. All whose loose talk tends toward putting the United States into a third world war, are in the dumb unconcern of the old lady at the garden party with a lion bouncing around twenty yards away.

Now, please do not write in to ask Simeon what he would do. He is not even the 29th Assistant Secretary of State. He is only asking for more deep concern and fewer cold sandwiches. His position is perfectly represented by a recent cartoon which shows a grim-faced customer confronting a clerk in a bookstore. The shelves behind the clerk are bulging with books whose titles show: *Mind at Rest, Don't Worry, How to be Happy*. The customer is asking: "Haven't you got something that won't give me cowlike complacency about the world? I want to be concerned, stimulated, stirred, worried . . ."

So may it be.

Yours,

SIMEON STYLITES.

What Is Your Fog Index?

Sir: Perhaps you did not know that you had a Fog Index. But Mr. Robert Gunning says that you have, and that it shows every time you open your mouth or write anything longer than your name. Your Fog Index is another number to carry around with you, in addition to your blood-pressure score, your driver's license, and your basic metabolism.

Your Fog Index, Mr. Gunning declares in his book *The Technique of Clear Writing,* is the point at which you go into low visibility in your effort to communicate meaning. If the clarity of your speech or writing resembles the fog off the Grand Banks of Newfoundland on a murky day, your Fog Index is high. If, on the other hand, you speak and write in a "This-is-a-cat" style, your Fog Index is low.

There is no doubt about the actuality of fog. It is a real and constant hazard in speech and writing; not only in party platforms and income-tax blanks (Form 1040) and the small print of insurance policies, but anywhere. I do not like to boast, but I can out-fog any contender of my weight in a ten-round bout.

Yet I am sure that Mr. Gunning's hocus-pocus, by which he arrives at his Readability Yardstick, is all cock-eyed. He gets the Fog Index by averaging the number of words in the sentences of a passage, then counting the number of words of three syllables or more in every 100 words, adding the two and multiplying by 4. On his scale, Lincoln's Gettysburg Address gets the crown with a low Fog Index of 10, *Harper's* magazine rates 15, John Milton 26. Surprisingly, Daniel Defoe turns out one of the most long-winded writers of English, averaging more than 50 words per sentence.

But this legerdemain makes the false assumption that short words and few words in a sentence dispel the fog. Nonsense! It is deeper than that. A foggy idea, clothed in short, stubby, one-syllabled words, can still be completely opaque, ceiling zero. And a version of Einstein's relativity done by Hans Christian Andersen for the First-Grade Primer would still be a very foggy night. Often the trouble is not in the words but in the general style. Thus someone once described Coleridge's writing as "lizard-like": "He slips lizard-like into a thicket of learned excerpts, and vanishes from sight, leaving in our hands his tail only."

Still, it might help to try Mr. Gunning's formula on some of your written stuff. The nature of fog is shown in the following report of official correspondence:

> A New York city plumber wrote to the Bureau of Standards in Washington saying that he had found hydrochloric acid good for cleaning out clogged drains. The bureau wrote him: "The efficacy of hydrochloric acid is indisputable, but the corrosive residue is incompatible with metallic

> permanence." The plumber replied that he was glad the bureau agreed with him. The bureau tried again, saying: "We cannot assume the responsibility for the production of toxic and noxious residue with hydrochloric acid, and suggest that you use an alternative procedure." The plumber again wrote that he was pleased the bureau agreed with him. Finally the bureau wrote to the plumber: "Don't use hydrochloric acid. It eats hell out of the pipes."

How about a cure? There you have me! You might try a fog horn. But a fog horn merely calls attention to the fog; it does nothing to dispel it. About a cure for fog, I — er-ah — well, you have guessed it: I am in a fog.

Murkily yours,

SIMEON STYLITES.

The Grace of Receiving

Sir: "It is more blessed to give than to receive." But it is a poor rule that won't work both ways. This one does. For it is also blessed to receive. Too many people forget that. The givers who cannot take in return miss one of the finest graces in life, the grace of receiving.

We all know the man who, no matter how outwardly generous, is too vain and self-important ever to receive a favor gratefully. That would put him on a level with the other person, and he always has to stand above the other person in one way or another, else his ego will be painfully deflated. When he dines with you — pardon me, that is wrong: *you* always dine with *him* — his reach for the check could never be described with the words, "as feeble as the struggle for a night-club check." There is no struggle. He takes it, with a generous gesture which indicates, "Don't kid yourself that you are my equal. I'm the Big Shot here. Get out of my way."

In her *Benefits Forgot,* G. B. Stern has drawn in sharp lines a picture of one-way givers:

> While we benefit by their largess, their way of standing treat without ostentation, but as though it could not be otherwise, we cannot help wondering what is fundamentally wrong, to account for their obvious reluctance to receive gifts, to receive hospitality, to let the other man pay for a change. And more than reluctance, their positive discomfort, their inability to show pleasure or utter words of thanks that are not churlish or unreal.

They have the delusion that accepting anything places them among the beggars.

Theirs is not an ostentatious splurge. It is deeper than that, and, so, worse. It is an ingrained habit which spoils things with a subtle poison. "We'll go in my car," with the unspoken implication, "(it is better than yours)." "I will buy the tickets (you can't afford to)." "Have dinner at my house (we serve better meals)."

The recognition of this lack goes clear back to the sharp-sighted boys among the ancients. Tacitus saw it: "Benefits are only so far acceptable as they appear capable of being returned; if they pass much beyond that limit, they reap hatred rather than gratitude."

The grace of receiving, of course, does not mean reaching out the tin cup of a panhandler to every passer-by. That is not a grace, but a disgrace. The daughters of the horseleech, who kept screaming "Give, give, give," are not to be confused with the Three Graces.

The grace of receiving is sharing with others the luxury of giving, and not always grasping to snatch it away from them. To receive gratefully from others is to enhance their sense of their worth. It puts them on a give-and-take level, the only level on which real fellowship can be sustained. Humble receiving smothers the strident clamor of self-insistence. It shrinks the swollen ego to size. It helps to make a Big Noise back into a human being. It changes one of the ugliest things in the world, patronage, into one of the richest things in the world, friendship. Why should we ever forget that in the most vital of all things, we are receivers from God of his love?

Yours,

SIMEON STYLITES.

The Inside Story

Sir: Have you noticed that 1954 has been the 100th anniversary of the publication of Thoreau's *Walden?* That merits a passing salute, at least. One item particularly, is worth recalling: the entry Henry Thoreau made in his journal on the day that *Walden* was published. Here it is: "August 9, 1854. Elderberries. *Walden* published. Waxwork (the false bittersweet) yellowing." There is something to look at! Elderberries and bittersweet were at least as important as his book. He could take a book in his stride and set it down in a casual manner. Quite an art!

Many of us — perhaps most of us — if we had just given a classic to the world, would have engaged a brass band, or at least a fife-and-drum corps, so that they might sound forth with "Hail to the Chief." That is just one little difference between most of us and Thoreau. Frequently, if we have had any accomplishment, such as being elected secretary of the Village Improvement Society or writing a letter to the newspaper, we become an Ancient Mariner, and buttonhole passers-by to give them a blow-by-blow description of the whole works.

Perhaps "taking it in your stride" is a mark of greatness. John Keats once wrote in a letter, when he was visiting: "I took some thin paper and wrote some verses. They are called The Eve of St. Agnes." Not a bad use for "thin paper." But Keats, like Thoreau, could take it in his stride.

The reason that Thoreau could link *Walden* casually with elderberries and bittersweet was that his awareness of the world of nature made the "inside story" of sensitive perception more important than any merely outside happenings. He was one of those happy mortals who can see that what goes on in the inside of the heart and mind is not only more worth while but also more exciting. So often the outside story swamps the inside story into Lilliputian proportions. As Carlyle remarked, we feel that the salutation "Good morning, Clothes," or "Good morning, Medals," is far more fitting than "Good morning, Soul."

A contemporary poet, Thomas Caldecott Chubb, has put this relative importance of the inside story of the soul over the outside story of clothes, medals and other items into a poem entitled "Biography." He asks his biographer not to set down that he lived in a certain place, wrote this book or that, or studied laboriously and learned this or that fact, but that he looked on the face of beauty

On such a moonlit night, or such a dawn
All diamonded with dew upon the lawn.

He cautions his biographer not to say what he did or thought,

But rather: "Here he heard the mockingbird,
Smelled the wistaria, saw the Cherokee rose."

We might celebrate the *Walden* centenary fittingly by asking ourselves how the inside story compares to the outside one. Some years ago a professional holy man of India, as a penance, added a large iron ring to his legs every year. Finally he got so heavy that the railroad refused to accept him as a passenger and classified him as freight. A great many people, if they were weighed by what they carry inside them, would go forward as freight.

Hoping you are not the same.

Yours,

SIMEON STYLITES.

The Devils Were White

Sir: The Ethiopian Church portrays all the saints as black and all the devils as white. We can readily understand the point of view. For that is not merely a bit of minor ecclesiastical lore, but just about the most important and terrifying fact of our time. Many of the devils in the world have been, and are, white devils.

Not, of course, by the white man's traditions of art. We do not make pictures of Satan with blond hair and blue eyes and a light skin. Once in a while, as in *Faust,* we give the devil a red suit, but that is just to liven up the scene. We never make him white.

The Ethiopian Church has a lot of history on its side. History is full of white devils. The long, revolting story of the African slave trade is a story of white devils. For centuries the forests of Africa rang with the cry, "Run for your lives! The white devils are coming!" They came, and in some years took away a hundred thousand slaves. It is hard to imagine what a stranglehold the slave trade had on the whole economy of Great Britain, before the advent of Wilberforce and Clarkson and others. It was as though a monster octopus had swum up the Mersey estuary, where most of the slave ships went out from, and spread its slimy tentacles to grasp every institution — Parliament, the banks, and many churches.

China knew the white devils all to well. In 1839 the Opium War was forced on China by Great Britain to sanction the importation of opium. The white devils wound the chains of opium on multitudes of Chinese, and then took Hong King for good measure. Shortly after, Christian missionaries began to carry Christian teachings to the heathen Chinese, who were so besotted as to object to opium. The real bill for all that began to come in back in the 1940's and 1950's. It is still coming in.

White devils are abroad in South Africa. Many of the worst of them are armed — as has sometimes happened — with a Bible. They are skillful devils, fomenters of chaos as accomplished in the oppression of the black people as any devils that ever took a postgraduate course in Hell. Langston Hughes has summed it up in a few words:

I'm looking for a house in the world
Where the white shadows
Will not fall.

There is no such house,
Dark brother,
No such house
At all.

In these days when we talk so much about the Ecumenical Church, one good step might be to come a bit closer to the Ethiopian Church and share its sharp vision of the color of devils. Perhaps we might arrange to have fewer white ones, at any rate.

Yours,

SIMEON STYLITES.

Broadcasting a Quaker Meeting

Sir: What would be your "dream" radio or television program? I thought so! Mine would be the same. I am fast coming to the feeling that my dream program would not be any kind of noise, clattering over the air waves, but silence. Silence that comes like a healing poultice on battered ears. That would be a lot better than the million-dollar messes frequently served up on TV, with much ado about nothing.

My dream program was announced some time ago, but alas, it came from England and I couldn't tune in on the B.B.C. It was the first broadcast of a Quaker Sunday morning service. That would be a program to tune in on — Quaker silence, which is not merely the absence of noise but a positive thing, a blessing. As Rose Macaulay wrote in gratitude for a Quaker meeting: "The Friends sit in stillness, waiting on the Spirit, who will presently move someone to rise and speak. For my own part, I shall not be ill-pleased should the Spirit move no one this morning, except the squirrels and the birds, and that distant hen who would appear to have produced an egg."

Simeon has always been an enemy of hysterical adjectives, and so he hates to call anything on radio or TV "colossal." But one thing surely richly deserves the adjective "colossal," and that is the impertinence of many commercials. The worst feature of commericals is not the imbecile earnestness of the hucksters plugging for the product. The worst feature is the new high achieved in recent years by cigarette and beer advertisers, a new high in insufferable intrusion into the home. The cigarette companies have been given sharp warning by the Communications Commission. The beer barons ought to be given a heave-ho by a million viewers and listeners. Baseball has been made hideous by the moronic repetition of the same worn-out plug every inning. And the poor announcer pouring out and drinking a glass of beer every inning, till by the seventh he looks groggy and more than half-seas over — that obscene spectacle comes right into our living rooms. Can't we revive that provision of the English common law that a man's house is his castle?

We need the Quaker meeting for other reasons. In so many ways we, as a people, have declared war on solitude and meditation. We are lost without a "set" or a "bunch." The worst possible calamity is to be alone. If you enjoy anything alone, you are "anti-social" and ought to be rushed to the psychoanalyst's couch, or better still to the mental hospital. A few years ago a woman knelt in prayer at noontime in the churchyard of St. Paul's Chapel on Broadway, New York. The shocked onlookers sent for the police wagon, which took her away. Anything so antisocial as private prayer obviously must be handled by the police! Norman Cousins has put it truly:

> Plainly this is not an age of meditative man. It is a squinting, sprinting, shoving age. Substitutes for repose are a million-dollar business. Silence, already the nation's most critical shortage, is almost a nasty word. Modern man may or may not be obsolete, but he is certainly wired for sound, and has ants in his pants.

Now, to complete the gloom, comes the promotion of the portable radio, so that a person may be in no danger of being a prey to his own thoughts. The portable radio is an outward and visible sign of the decline and fall of the mind.

O happy day, when we can tune in on a Quaker meeting, a sacrament of silence!

Yours,

SIMEON STYLITES.

"Take Me Out to the Ball Game"

Sir: You remember Browning's beautiful lines,

O to be in Wrigley Field
Now that the Cubs are there!

May I suggest that there is more on a baseball diamond than entertainment and excitement? The rousing spectacle of the boys running the bases has some real wisdom for any organization, and for the church in particular, if it can spare the time to stop, look, and listen to the crack of the bat.

The basic principle of a successful ball team is *the long look ahead* — the persistent search for new talent, for future strength, to be brought up four or five years in advance. If a high school boy, sixteen or seventeen years old, in Prairie View, Nebraska, strikes out eighteen players in a game, seven scouts from seven cities make an airplane trip to look him over and sign him up. No place is too small or insignificant to go to if there is a rumor of real potential ability.

The churches, in general, have had nothing like the same relentless concern for their future leadership. Following old traditions, they have been far too casual in trying to discover and sign up the best. There has been, and is, altogether too much complacent waiting for candidates to apply, rather than going out and getting the best.

The situation is better today than in other years.

No man has given a better demonstration of the effectiveness of strategic scouting for the church than has that pioneer in many realms, Bishop James C. Baker, of the Methodist Church in California. For over twenty years he has made an annual trip to seven or eight of the country's theological seminaries with the determination to build up strength for the years ahead. As a result, he has got together one of the finest teams of hard-hitting rookies to be found anywhere in the land.

One other thing is to be noticed about baseball — often in sharp contrast to the procedures of the church: that the one purpose of baseball owners and managers *is to win ball games.* If a man can do the job in superb fashion, he is put in, no matter who he is or where he comes from or how old he is. Consider Willie Mays, for instance, late of the New York Giants. Nineteen years old, picked up in "the sticks." He had everything against him, except one thing: he could play ball. In some conferences — some Methodist conferences, for instance — the district superintendents and the bishop would have said, "Now, Willie, you are young, only nineteen. Remember that there are many men who have been on the club for ten or twenty years or more. You sit here on the bench till you are thirty-five, or perhaps even only thirty, and then we will let you play in a game." So that, instead of having a large share in winning the pennant in 1951, Willie would have waited till 1961, and then been pushed out to bat in a wheelchair.

But the fanatics who run ball clubs are one-eyed men; they are interested not in seniority or the right connections but, strangely enough, in winning ball games.

Honest now, how many churches are there that are losing more games than they win because the ecclesiastical authorities are far more interested in "taking care of men" than in giving churches the strongest leadership possible for a winning fight?

Turn to hymn No. 104 and sing, "Take me out to the ball game."

Yours,

SIMEON STYLITES.

The Wail of a Duffer

Sir: Have you ever paused to shed a bitter tear over the distressing truth that most of the things we used to do for fun have been made so scientific that all the fun is knocked out of them? If you haven't wept over it, get some tears ready now.

Take my camera. Sure, you might as well take it. I can't work it. Remember how we used to take pictures just for fun? We simply grabbed the Brownie, either upside down or right side up, it made no difference, and went out and snapped pictures and had ourselves a time. Progress has changed all that. Picture-making is not fun any more, in which any duffer could join. It is now a project in higher mathematics and non-

Euclidean geometry. You can't just shoot. You have to pace off the distance as though you were going to fight a duel. You have to be sure the shutter speed and the light speed and the normal arrow synchronize. It is as simple as calculus. All you have to do is ascertain the film speed from the little Ph.D. thesis which comes with the camera, and then press button C and move tab X until the Weston speed of the film appears in the window Y. I told you it was simple. After you get the gang posing on the steps and all saying "Cheese," all you have to do is to set the control dial to the light value obtained on the light scale, say "Abracadabra," and turn on any combination of the F stop and shutter speed, then open the "baffle." I always get baffled before I get started. The world is not safe for duffers who just want some fun. Probably we should be ashamed of ourselves.

Remember, we used to play a game called by a quaint old-fashioned name, "whist." It was played with cards; you slapped down a card when it came your turn. How we used to laugh! It was a lot of fun, so of course it was knocked out by science. Now the highbrows play — if that is the word — "contract," beside which analytical geometry is a pastime for moppets. When you play you are vulnerable, at least to a splitting headache. It is played by fanatics who would threaten to slip a dagger into you if you overbid your hand. I suppose for an ordinary amateur who only wants the fun of a game, there is nothing left in its natural state but Canasta. However, we shall soon have that invaded by science and there will be nasty Canasta experts.

Time would fail me to tell of golf as it was before the scientists and experts cleared it of all contamination of old-fashioned fun. We used to have a whale of a time doing nine holes in a hundred strokes or so. Now, with its "nineteen things wrong with your stance" and about twenty-two clubs to be pushed around the course in a perambulator, it is a branch of advanced science. And even croquet has suffered a change. It is usually "roque," played with a sextant, surveying instruments, short clubs, and short tempers.

Can't the world be made safe for duffers who don't want to be champions but are just out for fun? Surely I am not the only one. Will we be reduced to the only games that cannot be ruined by scientific skill — dominoes and hop, step, and jump? And oh, yes, let's have a game of parchesi!

Gloomily yours,

SIMEON STYLITES.

New Christian Symbols

Sir: The pastor of St. John's-by-the-Gas-Station dropped in the other day to solicit a subscription to the new stained-glass windows he wants to put in the church. He came right to the point.

"If you folks will loosen up as you ought to," he

said, "we are not only going to have new windows, but a lot of new Christian symbols on them. There are a lot of animals left in the zoo that we haven't touched yet. Of course we have the lamb and the eagle and the dove. But there are a lot more good ones.

"How about the pig, for instance? Don't grunt! He is a noble animal. More than that, the quality of the pig was one of the first things noticed sharply by the pagans in the first century. Remember good old Pliny in his letter to Tacitus? Here it is — what he wrote about the Christians: 'But, innocent as their practice may be, their obstinacy in asserting absurd beliefs, when I reasoned with them, sorely tried the patience of an amiable Roman gentleman. Pigheadedness like that really does call down punishment.' Great Scott, what a tribute! We need more pigheadedness. The folks in St. John's could stand a big shot of it. Most of the time, when somebody steps on them, instead of getting pigheaded they say, 'Pardon us, our mistake, excuse it please!'

"Take the inchworm. Boy, there is a symbol for the church! Did you ever watch one? He lifts up his head for a reconnoiter, then a lunge forward, then he pulls the rest of him up to consolidate his position. Then another lift of the head for another survey, and the same thing over again. The inchworm is the most undiscourageable animal on earth. I don't know how he will look in stained glass. He hasn't got much glamor. But he has what we need.

"We are going to have a window for another worm

that is a good symbol, the bookworm. He is a good symbol for devotion to books — he lives in them. Any church needs more bookworms — that is, folks who live in the Bible. It was a wise man who said during the homage to the Revised Standard Version of the Bible that what we need is 'Revised Readers' — people who actually read the Bible. Too many of our folks are like the man in one of Dean Charles R. Brown's stories, who thanked his pastor for a sermon on the geography of the Holy Land. 'For the first time,' he said gratefully, 'I realized that Dan and Beersheba were places. I always thought they were man and wife, like Sodom and Gomorrah.' Even when our folks know a few names they get them as mixed up as the girl in the history class who wrote on her examination paper: 'Molly Pitcher was the wife of a Revolutionary soldier who, when her husband was shot, took his place at the cannon and said, "Shoot if you must this old gray head, but I propose to fight it out on this line if it takes all summer." '

"Remember that they used to call the early Methodists at Oxford 'Bible moths'? Who would call any of us Bible moths today? How about a Society for the Recovery of Old Taunts? That might get us somewhere. How much shall we put you down for on the windows?"

That's what he said.

Yours,

SIMEON STYLITES.

Do-It-Yourself

Sir: Eternal vigilance is the price of liberty. It is high time for the tocsin to ring out, calling all husbands to the defense of the American home. I do not know what a tocsin is, but I'm ringing it anyhow.

The most vicious and insidious attack on the rights of American husbands and the peace of the home is the "Do-It-Yourself" movement which is sweeping the country at an appalling rate. The idea is to keep the head of the house busy every spare moment of the year making some fool repairs or so-called "improvements" around the house.

Woodrow Wilson said in immortal words, "The history of freedom is the history of resistance." So here is a blow for freedom. We need a Resistance Movement!

The whole thing evidently comes from collusion between restless wives, eager to have some sort of chaos going on, and hardware merchants. It is promoted by diabolical pictures in the magazines showing agile steeple jacks putting a new flashing on the chimney or shingling the roof or making a set of screens, always with a moronic grin on their faces.

The movement is really moving. The barons of the paint business gleefully announce that in 1953 paint sales gained a hundred million dollars over 1952 and that "the home craftsman is primarily responsible for the increase."

Now cities are starting "do-it-yourself" expositions,

at which all sorts of instruments of torture for meditative husbands are displayed. The police ought to suppress them. Propaganda catalogues of homecraft power tools flood the country. Pictures show a bird-brained husband slaving over a circular saw and jointer combination in the cellar, with the wife in the cheering section urging him on. A truer picture would be one showing the oaf falling off the roof or upsetting a bucket of paint on his head.

This is an attack on the fundamental liberties of the key person in our American culture, the head of the house. After a hard day's work at the office or store or baseball park shall we come home to a bombardment of "do-it-yourself" propaganda, with a display of tools and supplies?

You can see what this is doing to the home. Its peace is gone. The loving wife no longer runs and gets the slippers when you get home; she runs and gets the trowel, the paint brush, and the stepladder! It makes for alienation of affections, too. The ideal of American womanhood is no longer the thoughtful, contemplative executive, such as yourself, but some weak-minded Handy Andy who has no more to do than lay cement walks, simonize the car, and paint the garage. When the wife sees one of them she thinks, "I wish I had married one of those!" As though the divorce rate were not high enough as it is!

This movement has gone far enough. If you put in all your time at do-it-yourself pranks, why do it? Perhaps one hope would be to call in the labor unions. I have never been a fan for Mr. Petrillo, but I can see that a tsar in the home repair field might do wonders for freedom. Then any worm who allowed himself to be goaded by his wife into a do-it-youself stunt would have his gas and electricity shut off by sympathetic strikes.

But it is much better in this case to do-it-yourself without benefit of any Petrillo. Just go out in the back yard and practice saying "No!" Strike for your altars and your fires! And made it a sitdown strike! There is a better motto than "do-it-yourself." It is an old one, but good — "Let George do it!"

Yours,

SIMEON STYLITES.

Christmas Roses

Sir: There they are. There is no doubt about it. Incredible, but true. Christmas roses, blooming in a bed of snow! Ever-green leaves and ever-blooming flowers — white, shaped like a wild rose. People going by stop and gaze with wide-eyed astonishment. The roses have absolutely no business to be there! But they are no optical illusion. Astonishing!

That astonishment of people stopped on the sidewalk is a symbol of one of the great gifts of Christmas: its quickening of the capacity for astonishment. That is a gift desperately needed in a world where the capacity for amazement is becoming more and more depleted. The decline of the ability to wonder, to be astonished, is partly the result of the tragedy of growing up, of losing much of that rich fund of curiosity with which the child is endowed.

A. A. Milne pictured alluringly the child's inheritance of wonder when he wrote of a boy's reeling off a list of amazing things he could see while out for a walk: sun on river and hill; the sound of the sea "if you stand quite still"; new puppies at a near-by farm; most awe-inspiring of all, an old sailor with an empty sleeve. But — there were the grown-ups standing quite still instead of jumping with joy, able only to admonish: "Run along, run along."

Oldsters can so easily become a Society for the Suppression of Astonishment. The vision splendid in the child's eye so often fades into the light of very common day. So it is fitting that Christmas, the festival of the Child, should bring the gift of astonishment restored.

The Christmas story began with wonder. The shepherds were "sore afraid." That is, they were stunned with astonishment. The whole affair was fantastic. Chesterton sensed the very genius of the Day: "the things that cannot be and are."

And how sorely we need an increased ability to wonder! Ours is a world surfeited with facts and information and entertainment, but deficient in wonder. We have an unceasing parade of novelties, but a "rapidity of things going stale." It is one of the strange paradoxes of our time that a world full of wonders has lost the sense of wonder. The two are quite different. We gape at a bewildering succession of marvelous machines, but there is little of the deep amazement felt on the Judean hills so long ago: "When I consider the heavens, the work of thy fingers, the moon and the stars which thou hast ordained." One reason religion to so many becomes stale, flat, and wearisome is that the sheer wonder is left out.

Increasingly we live in a push-button world: no surprises, no fantastic wonders; just common sense, which gets to be as stale as the "remainder biscuit after a voyage." But Christmas knocks a routine world of order topsy-turvy. Everything is gloriously out of place: a song in the sky, a baby in a barn. That out-of-placeness brings astonishment to lives needing badly the thrill of wonder. For life is truly measured not by the number of breaths taken, but by the number not taken, the occasions when breath is stopped in amazement. This is the breath-taking astonishment of Christmas.

Christmas roses — a root out of dry ground, the Day-spring from on high — that is enough astonishment for one day, and for all days.

And many of them to you,

SIMEON STYLITES.